The Myth of Freedom

and the Way of Meditation

by Chögyam Trungpa

Edited by John Baker and Marvin Casper
Illustrated by Glen Eddy

THE CLEAR LIGHT SERIES

Shambhala

BOULDER & LONDON

1976

SHAMBHALA PUBLICATIONS, INC.
1920 13th Street
Boulder, CO 80302

© 1976 Chögyam Trungpa
Illustrations © 1976 Shambhala Publications, Inc.
All Rights Reserved

ISBN 0-87773-084-9
LCC 75-40264
Designed by Hal Hershey
Printed in the United States of America

This book is published in THE CLEAR LIGHT SERIES
dedicated to W. Y. Evans-Wentz. The series is
edited by Samuel Bercholz.

12 11 10 9 8 7 6 5

The Myth of Freedom

This book is dedicated to Dorje Tröllo,
the Crazy Wisdom form of Padmasambhava,
the father and protector of all beings.

Contents

Illustrations

1. *His Holiness the XVI Gyalwang Karmapa.* Gyalwang Karmapa is the supreme head of the Kagyü order of Tibetan Buddhism. He is the embodiment of the power and compassion of Buddhist tantra. He currently resides at Rumtek Abbey in Sikkim, India. He is a friend and inspiration to the author. *Page xii.*

2. *Milarepa with Vajrayogini above his head.* Milarepa, one of the founding fathers of the Kagyü lineage, is renowned for having attained enlightenment in one lifetime. His life serves as an example of the approach of the yogi in Tibetan Buddhism, combining asceticism with devotion. Thus his followers are known as Kagyüpas, the practising lineage. Above his head is Vajrayogini who represents the feminine aspect of one's innate nature and the clarity gained from discriminating awareness. The Vajrayogini principle plays an important role in the Kagyü tradition. *Page 42.*

3. *Four-armed Mahakala.* Described on pages 79-80 in the text. *Page 60.*

4. *Klong-chen rab-byams-pa (Longchenpa) with Shri Singha above his head.* Longchenpa was a great teacher of the Nyingma lineage of Tibetan Buddhism. He is known for systematizing the oral teachings of this lineage. Shri Singha was an Indian master of the highest teachings of tantra. He was a teacher of Padmasambhava, who brought the buddha-dharma to Tibet. *Page 100.*

5. *Vajradhara.* The Buddha manifests himself as Vajradhara to expound the teachings of tantra. He is also the supreme buddha expressing the whole of existence as un-

born and unoriginated. The tantric practitioner's personal teacher is identified with Vajradhara. He is the source of several important lineages of Buddhism in Tibet. *Page 126.*

6. *Mandala of the five buddha-wisdoms.* These are the basic attributes of how enlightened mind perceives and manifests in the phenomenal world through the manner of the five wisdoms: wisdom of all-encompassing space, mirror-like wisdom, wisdom of equanimity, discriminating-awareness wisdom, and wisdom of accomplishing all actions. *Page 146.*

7. *Ekajati with Samantabhadra above her head.* Ekajati is a protectress of the dharma and guide to the masters of tantric teachings. She is a destroyer of those who pervert the true meaning of the dharma. Samantabhadra is the primordial buddha who represents the final state of wakefulness. *Page 164.*

Preface

THE MYTH OF FREEDOM is based on lectures given by Chögyam Trungpa, Rinpoche in various parts of the United States between 1971 and 1973. The enormous interest in Trungpa's previous book, *Cutting Through Spiritual Materialism,* has inspired us to present another set of his lectures in book form. *The Myth of Freedom* can be viewed as a companion volume to *Cutting Through* or as an independent introduction to the Buddhist psychology and meditative practice of Tibet.

The book is flanked in the front by an original poem by Chögyam Trungpa which describes the stages of the spiritual path and in back by Trungpa's translation of a classic text, Tilopa's instructions on Mahamudra meditation to his disciple Naropa. The text seemed particularly appropriate since Tilopa was the father of Trungpa's eleven-hundred-year-old Kagyu lineage.

Enthronement

ONE

Parents are very kind,
But I am too young to appreciate it.
The highland mountains and valleys are beautiful,
But having never seen the lowlands, I am stupid.

TWO

Having striven for mind's nourishment,
Sharpening the spearhead of intellect,
I discovered permanent parents
Whom I can never forget.

THREE

Having no one to influence my outlook,
I display my primordial nature
And adopt the style of a youthful prince.
This is due to the only father guru.

FOUR

I am busy working for others.
Prajna, penetrating all obstacles,
Has made the prince old and wise,
Fearing no one.

FIVE

Dancing in space,
Clad in clouds,
Eating the sun and holding the moon,
The stars are my retinue.

SIX

The naked child is beautiful and dignified.
The red flower blooms in the sky.
It is ironic to see the formless dancer,
Dancing to the trumpet without a trumpeter.

SEVEN

At the palace of red ruby,
Listening to the utterance of the seed syllable,
It is joyful to watch the dance of illusion,
The seductive maidens of phenomena.

EIGHT

The warrior without a sword,
Riding on a rainbow,
Hears the limitless laughter of transcendent joy.
The poisonous snake becomes amrita.

NINE

Drinking fire, wearing water,
Holding the mace of the wind,
Breathing earth,
I am the lord of the three worlds.

January 22, 1973

I
The Myth of
Freedom

Fantasy and Reality

IF WE ARE to plant the complete Buddhist teachings in American soil we must first understand the fundamental principles of Buddhism and work through its basic meditation practices. Many people respond to Buddhism as if it were a new cult which might save them, which might enable them to deal with the world in the manner of picking flowers in a beautiful garden. But if we wish to pick flowers from a tree, we must first cultivate the roots and trunk, which means that we must work with our fears, frustrations, disappointments and irritations, the painful aspects of life.

People complain that Buddhism is an extremely gloomy religion because it emphasizes suffering and misery. Usually religions speak of beauty, song, ecstasy, bliss. But according to Buddha, we must begin by seeing the experience of life as it is. We must see the truth of suffering, the reality of dissatisfaction. We cannot ignore it and attempt to examine only the glorious, pleasurable aspects of life. If one searches for a promised land, a Treasure Island, then the search only leads to more pain. We cannot reach such islands, we cannot attain enlightenment in such a manner. So all sects and schools of Buddhism agree that we must begin by facing the reality

1

of our living situations. We cannot begin by dreaming. That would be only a temporary escape; real escape is impossible.

In Buddhism, we express our willingness to be realistic through the practice of meditation. Meditation is not a matter of trying to achieve ecstasy, spiritual bliss or tranquility, nor is it attempting to become a better person. It is simply the creation of a space in which we are able to expose and undo our neurotic games, our self-deceptions, our hidden fears and hopes. We provide space through the simple discipline of doing nothing. Actually, doing nothing is very difficult. At first, we must begin by approximating doing nothing, and gradually our practice will develop. So meditation is a way of churning out the neuroses of mind and using them as part of our practice. Like manure, we do not throw our neuroses away, but we spread them on our garden; they become part of our richness.

In meditation practice, we neither hold the mind very tightly nor let it go completely. If we try to control the mind, then its energy will rebound back on us. If we let the mind go completely, then it will become very wild and chaotic. So we let the mind go, but at the same time there is some discipline involved. The techniques used in the Buddhist tradition are extremely simple. Awareness of bodily movement, breath and one's physical situation are techniques common to all traditions. The basic practice is to be present, right here. The goal is also the technique. Precisely being in this moment, neither suppressing nor wildly letting go, but being precisely aware of what you are. Breath, like bodily existence, is a neutral process which has no "spiritual" connotations. We simply become mindful of its natural functioning. This is called *shamatha* practice. With this practice we begin to tread the *hinayana* or narrow path. This is not to say that the hinayana approach is simplistic or narrow-minded. Rather, because the mind is so complicated, so exotic, craving all sorts of entertainment constantly, the only way to deal with it is to channel it into a disciplined path without sidetracks. The hinayana is a vehicle which does not speed, one which is right on the point, a vehicle which does not get sidetracked. We have no opportunity to run away; we are right here and cannot step out. It is a vehicle without a reverse gear. And the simplicity of narrowness also brings an open attitude toward life situations, because we realize that there is no escape of any kind and give in to being right on the spot.

So we acknowledge what we are rather than try to hide from our problems and irritations. Meditation should not help you forget your commitment at the office. In fact, in the practice of sitting meditation you relate to your daily life all the time. Meditation practice brings our neuroses to the surface rather than hiding them at the bottom of our minds. It enables us to relate to our lives as something workable. I think people have the idea that, if only they could get away from the hustle and bustle of life, then they could really get into some sort of contemplative practice up in the mountains or at the seashore. But escaping the mundanity of our lives is to neglect the food, the actual nourishment which exists between two layers of bread. When you order a sandwich, you do not order two layers of bread. You have something in the middle which is chunky, eatable, delicious, and the bread comes along with it.

Then becoming more clearly aware of emotions and

life situations and the space in which they occur might
open us to a still more panoramic awareness. A compassionate attitude, a warmth, develops at this point. It is
an attitude of fundamental acceptance of oneself while
still retaining critical intelligence. We appreciate the
joyful aspect of life along with the painful aspect. Relating to emotions ceases to be a big deal. Emotions are
as they are, neither suppressed nor indulged but simply
acknowledged. So the precise awareness of details leads
into an openness to the complex totality of situations.
Like a great river that runs down toward the ocean, the
narrowness of discipline leads into the openness of panoramic awareness. Meditation is not purely sitting alone
in a particular posture attending to simple processes, but
is also an openness to the environment in which these
processes take place. The environment becomes a reminder to us, continually giving us messages, teachings,
insights.

So before we indulge in any exotic techniques, playing with energies, playing with sense perceptions, playing with visions in terms of religious symbolism, we
must sort out our minds fundamentally. We must begin
our practice by walking the narrow path of simplicity,
the hinayana path, before we can walk upon the open
highway of compassionate action, the *mahayana* path.
And only after our highway journey is well on its way
need we concern ourselves about how to dance in the
fields—the *vajrayana* or *tantric* teachings. The simplicity
of the hinayana is the foundation for appreciating the
splendor of the mahayana and the tremendous color of
tantra. So before we relate with heaven we must relate
to earth and work on our basic neuroses. The whole
approach of Buddhism is to develop transcendental com-

mon sense, seeing things as they are, without magnifying what is or dreaming about what we would like to be.

Disappointment

As LONG AS we follow a spiritual approach promising salvation, miracles, liberation, then we are bound by the "golden chain of spirituality." Such a chain might be beautiful to wear, with its inlaid jewels and intricate carvings, but nevertheless, it imprisons us. People think they can wear the golden chain for decoration without being imprisoned by it, but they are deceiving themselves. As long as one's approach to spirituality is based upon enriching ego, then it is spiritual materialism, a suicidal process rather than a creative one.

All the promises we have heard are pure seduction. We expect the teachings to solve all our problems; we expect to be provided with magical means to deal with our depressions, our aggressions, our sexual hangups. But to our surprise we begin to realize that this is not going to happen. It is very disappointing to realize that we must work on ourselves and our suffering rather than depend upon a savior or the magical power of yogic techniques. It is disappointing to realize that we have to give up our expectations rather than build on the basis of our preconceptions.

We must allow ourselves to be disappointed, which means the surrendering of me-ness, my achievement. We

would like to watch ourselves attain enlightenment,
watch our disciples celebrating, worshipping, throwing
flowers at us, with miracles and earthquakes occurring
and gods and angels singing and so forth. This never
happens. The attainment of enlightenment from ego's
point of view is extreme death, the death of self, the
death of me and mine, the death of the watcher. It is the
ultimate and final disappointment. Treading the spiritual path is painful. It is a constant unmasking, peeling
off of layer after layer of masks. It involves insult after
insult.

Such a series of disappointments inspires us to give up
ambition. We fall down and down and down, until we
touch the ground, until we relate with the basic sanity of
earth. We become the lowest of the low, the smallest of
the small, a grain of sand, perfectly simple, no expectations. When we are grounded, there is no room for
dreaming or frivolous impulse, so our practice at last
becomes workable. We begin to learn how to make a
proper cup of tea, how to walk straight without tripping.
Our whole approach to life becomes more simple and
direct, and any teachings we might hear or books we
might read become workable. They become confirma-
tions, encouragements to work as a grain of sand, as we
are, without expectations, without dreams.

We have heard so many promises, have listened to so
many alluring descriptions of exotic places of all kinds,
have seen so many dreams, but from the point of view
of a grain of sand, we could not care less. We are just a
speck of dust in the midst of the universe. At the same
time our situation is very spacious, very beautiful and
workable. In fact, it is very inviting, inspiring. If you
are a grain of sand, the rest of the universe, all the space,

all the room is yours, because you obstruct nothing, over-crowd nothing, possess nothing. There is tremendous openness. You are the emperor of the universe because you are a grain of sand. The world is very simple and at the same time very dignified and open, because your inspiration is based upon disappointment, which is without the ambition of the ego.

Suffering

WE BEGIN OUR spiritual journey by asking questions, by doubting our deceptions. There is continual uncertainty as to what is real and unreal, what is happiness and what is misery. We experience this moment by moment and year by year as our lives unfold. We keep on asking questions and eventually the questions turn sour and begin to rot. They turn into pain. Pain increases as the questions become more solid and the answers more elusive.

As we grow older, in one way or another we begin to ask, "What is the meaning of life?" We might say, "What isn't the meaning of life? Everything is life." But that is too cute, too clever, and the question still remains. We could say that the meaning of life is to exist. Again, exist for what? What are we trying to achieve by leading our lives? Some people say that the meaning of life is to put our effort and energy toward higher goals: commuting between the earth and moon or becoming enlightened, becoming a great professor, great scientist, great mystic, to improve the world, clean up the earth's pollution. Maybe that is the meaning of life—that we are supposed to work hard and achieve something. We should discover wisdom and share it with others. Or we should create a better political order, reinforcing democracy so that all men are equal and everyone has a right to do whatever he wants within the limits of mutual responsibility. Perhaps we should raise the level of our civilization to the highest point so that our world becomes a fantastic place, a seat of wisdom, of enlightenment, of learning and the highest technological developments. There should be plenty to eat, pleasant houses, amiable company. We should become sophisticated, rich and happy, without quarrels, war or poverty, with tremendously powerful intellects that know all the answers, the scientific explanations of how the jellyfish began and how the cosmos operates.

I am not mocking this mentality, not at all, but have we considered the significance of death? The counterpart of life is death. Have we considered that? The very message of death is painful. If you were to ask your fifteen-year-old child to write his will, people would regard that as being completely absurd. No one would do that. We refuse to acknowledge death, but our highest ideals, our speculations on the meaning of life, the highest forms of civilization—all are impractical if we do not consider the process of birth, suffering and death.

From moment to moment, birth, suffering and death take place. Birth is opening into a new situation. Immediately after birth, there is the sense of refreshment, freshness, like watching the sun rise in the early morning. The birds begin to wake up and sing their songs, the air is fresh, we begin to see the hazy silhouettes of the trees and mountains. As the sun rises, the world becomes clearer and more defined. We watch the sun become redder and redder, finally turning into white light, bright sunshine. One would prefer to hold on to the dawn and sunrise, to keep the sun from rising completely, to hold on to the glowing promise. We would prefer to do this, but we cannot. No one has ever achieved it. We struggle to maintain the new situation, but finally we cannot hold on to anything and we are dead. When we die, there is a gap between the death and the next birth; but still that gap is filled with all kinds of subconscious gossip, questions as to what we should do, and we latch on to a new situation and are born again. We repeat this process again and again and again.

From this point of view, when you give birth to a child, if you really want to cling to life, you should not cut the umbilical cord as he is born. But you must. Birth is an expression of the separateness between mother and child. Either you are going to witness your child's death or the child is going to witness your death. Perhaps this is a very grim way of looking at life, but still it is true. Every move we make is an expression of birth, suffering and death.

There are three categories of suffering or pain in the Buddhist tradition: all-pervading pain, the pain of alternation and the pain of pain. All-pervading pain is the general pain of dissatisfaction, separation and loneliness. We are alone, we are lonely people, we cannot regenerate our umbilical cord, we cannot say of our birth that "it was a rehearsal." It has already happened. So pain is inevitable as long as there is the presence of discontinuity and insecurity.

All-pervading pain is general frustration resulting from aggression. Whether you are polite or blunt, a seemingly happy or unhappy person, is irrelevant. As long as we try to hold on to our existence, we become a bundle of tense muscles protecting ourselves. This creates discomfort. We tend to feel that our existence is slightly inconvenient. Even if we are self-contained and have plenty of money, food, shelter, companionship, still there is this little thing in our being which is in the way. Something is protruding from which we constantly have to shield and hide ourselves. We have to be watchful in case we goof up, but we are uncertain as to what we are going to goof up. There is a sort of universal understanding that there is something we must keep secret, something we should not goof up, something unnameable. It is not logical, but there is still some sort of threat.

So fundamentally, no matter how happy we may be, we are still careful and angry. We do not really want to be exposed, we do not really want to encounter this thing, whatever it is. Of course we could attempt to rationalize this feeling saying, "I didn't get enough sleep last night so I feel funny today and don't want to do difficult work—I might goof up." But such self-justifications are not valid. The concern over goofing up involves being angry as well as hiding. We are angry at the unnameable private parts that we do not want exposed. "If only I could get rid of this thing, then I would be relieved, I would feel free."

This fundamental pain takes innumerable forms—the pain of losing a friend, the pain of having to attack an enemy, the pain of making money, the pain of wanting credentials, the pain of washing dishes, the pain of duty, the pain of feeling that someone is watching over your shoulder, the pain of thinking that we haven't been efficient or successful, the pain of relationships of all kinds.

In addition to all-pervading pain, there is the pain of alternation, which is realizing that you are carrying a burden. Sometimes you begin to feel that the burden has disappeared because you feel free, that you do not have to keep up with yourself anymore. But the sense of alternation between pain and its absence, between sanity and insanity, again and again, is itself painful. Shouldering the burden again is very painful.

And then there is the pain of pain, which is the third type. You are already insecure, feeling uncertain about your territory. On top of that you worry about your condition and develop an ulcer. While rushing to the doctor to treat the ulcer you stub your toe. Resisting pain only increases its intensity. The three types of pain quickly follow one another in life, they pervade life. First you feel fundamental pain, and then the pain of alternation, from pain to its absence and back again; and then you have the pain of pain, the pain of all those life situations you do not want.

You decide to take a vacation in Paris, planning to have a good time, but something goes wrong. Your longtime French friend had an accident. He is in the hospital and his family is very upset, unable to provide you with the hospitality you had expected. Instead you have to stay in a hotel, which you cannot afford, as your money is running out. You decide to change your money on the black market and you get swindled. And your supposed friend, who had an accident and is in the hospital, suddenly starts to dislike you, begins to regard you as a nuisance. You want to return home, but you can't. All flights are cancelled because of bad weather. You are

really desperate. Every hour, every second is important
to you. You are pacing up and down in the airport and
your visa is running out. You have to get out of the
country soon. And explaining to the officials is very difficult because you do not speak French.

Such situations occur all the time. We are speeding,
trying to get rid of our pain, and we find more pain by
doing so. Pain is very real. We cannot pretend that we
are all happy and secure. Pain is our constant companion.
It goes on and on—all-pervading pain, the pain of alternation and the pain of pain. If we are seeking eternity or
happiness or security, then the experience of life is one
of pain, *duhkha,* suffering.

Egolessness

THE EFFORT TO secure our happiness, to maintain
ourselves in relation to something else, is the process of
ego. But this effort is futile because there are continual
gaps in our seemingly solid world, continual cycles of
death and rebirth, constant change. The sense of continuity and solidity of self is an illusion. There is really
no such thing as ego, soul or *atman.* It is a succession of
confusions that create ego. The process which is ego actually consists of a flicker of confusion, a flicker of aggression, a flicker of grasping—all of which exist only in the
moment. Since we cannot hold on to the present moment,
we cannot hold on to me and mine and make them solid
things.

The experience of oneself relating to other things is actually a momentary discrimination, a fleeting thought. If we generate these fleeting thoughts fast enough, we can create the illusion of continuity and solidity. It is like watching a movie, the individual film frames are played so quickly that they generate the illusion of continual movement. So we build up an idea, a preconception, that self and other are solid and continuous. And once we have this idea, we manipulate our thoughts to confirm it, and are afraid of any contrary evidence. It is this fear of exposure, this denial of impermanence that imprisons us. It is only by acknowledging impermanence that there is the chance to die and the space to be reborn and the possibility of appreciating life as a creative process.

There are two stages to understanding egolessness. In the first stage we perceive that ego does not exist as a solid entity, that it is impermanent, constantly changing, that it was our concepts that made it seem solid. So we conclude that ego does not exist. But we still have formulated a subtle concept of egolessness. There is still a watcher of the egolessness, a watcher to identify with it and maintain his existence. The second stage is seeing through this subtle concept and dropping the watcher. So true egolessness is the absence of the concept of egolessness. In the first stage there is a sense of someone perceiving egolessness. In the second, even the perceiver does not exist. In the first, we perceive that there is no fixed entity because everything is relative to something else. In the second stage there is the understanding that the notion of relativity needs a watcher to perceive it, to confirm it, which introduces another relative notion, the watcher and the watched.

To say that egolessness does exist because things are

constantly changing is quite feeble, since we still hold
on to change as something solid. Egolessness is not simply
the idea that, since there is discontinuity, therefore there
is nothing to hang on to. True egolessness involves the
non-existence of the discontinuity as well. We cannot
hang on to the idea of discontinuity either. In fact, discontinuity really does not operate. Our perception of
discontinuity is the product of insecurity; it is concept.
So too is any idea about the oneness behind or within
phenomena.

The idea of egolessness has often been used to obscure
the reality of birth, suffering and death. The problem is
that, once we have a notion of egolessness and a notion
of pain, birth and death, then we can easily entertain or
justify ourselves by saying that pain does not exist because there is no ego to experience it, that birth and
death do not exist because there is no one to witness
them. This is just cheap escapism. The philosophy of
shunyata has often been distorted by the presentation of
the idea that: "There is no one to suffer, so who cares?
If you suffer, it must be your illusion." This is pure
opinion, speculation. We can read about it, we can think
about it, but when we actually suffer, can we remain in-
different? Of course not; suffering is stronger than our
petty opinions. A true understanding of egolessness cuts
through opinion. The absence of a notion of egolessness
allows us to fully experience pain, birth and death because then there are no philosophical paddings.

The whole idea is that we must drop all reference
points, all concepts of what is or what should be. Then
it is possible to experience the uniqueness and vividness
of phenomena directly. There is tremendous room to
experience things, to allow experience to occur and pass

away. Movement happens within vast space. Whatever happens, pleasure and pain, birth and death and so forth, are not interfered with but are experienced in their fullest flavor. Whether they are sweet or sour, they are experienced completely, without philosophical over-lays or emotional attitudes to make things seem lovable or presentable.

We are never trapped in life, because there are con-stant opportunities for creativity, challenges for impro-visation. Ironically, by seeing clearly and acknowledging our egolessness, we may discover that suffering contains bliss, impermanence contains continuity or eternity and egolessness contains the earth quality of solid being. But this transcendental bliss, continuity and beingness is not based on fantasies, ideas or fears.

II
Styles of
Imprisonment

Cosmic Joke

IN ORDER TO cut through the ambition of ego, we must understand how we set up me and my territory, how we use our projections as credentials to prove our existence. The source of the effort to confirm our solidity is an uncertainty as to whether or not we exist. Driven by this uncertainty, we seek to prove our own existence by finding a reference point outside ourselves, something with which to have a relationship, something solid to feel separate from. But the whole enterprise is questionable if we really look back and back and back. Perhaps we have perpetrated a gigantic hoax?

The hoax is the sense of the solidity of I and other. This dualistic fixation comes from nothingness. In the beginning there is open space, zero, self-contained, without relationship. But in order to confirm zeroness, we must create one to prove that zero exists. But even that is not enough; we might get stuck with just one and zero. So we begin to advance, venture out and out. We create two to confirm one's existence, and then we go out again and confirm two by three, three by four and so on. We set up a background, a foundation from which we can go on and on to infinity. This is what is called *samsara*, the continuous vicious cycle of confirmation of existence. One confirmation needs another confirmation needs another . . .

The attempt to confirm our solidity is very painful. Constantly we find ourselves suddenly slipping off the edge of a floor which had appeared to extend endlessly. Then we must attempt to save ourselves from death by immediately building an extension to the floor in order to make it appear endless again. We think we are safe on our seemingly solid floor, but then we slip off again and have to build another extension. We do not realize that the whole process is unnecessary, that we do not need a floor to stand on, that we have been building all these floors on the ground level. There was never any danger of falling or need for support. In fact, our occupation of extending the floor to secure our ground is a big joke, the biggest joke of all, a cosmic joke. But we may not find it funny: it may sound like a serious double cross.

To understand more precisely the process of confirming the solidity of I and other, that is, the development of ego, it is helpful to be familiar with the five *skandhas,* a set of Buddhist concepts which describe ego as a five-step process.

The first step or skandha, the birth of ego, is called "form" or basic ignorance. We ignore the open, fluid, intelligent quality of space. When a gap or space occurs in our experience of mind, when there is a sudden glimpse of awareness, openness, absence of self, then a suspicion arises: "Suppose I find that there is no solid me? That possibility scares me. I don't want to go into that." That abstract paranoia, the discomfort that something may be wrong, is the source of karmic chain reactions. It is the fear of ultimate confusion and despair.

The fear of the absence of self, of the egoless state, is a constant threat to us. "Suppose it is true, what then? I am afraid to look." We want to maintain some solidity but the only material available with which to work is space, the absence of ego, so we try to solidify or freeze that experience of space. Ignorance in this case is not stupidity, but it is a kind of stubbornness. Suddenly we are bewildered by the discovery of selflessness and do not want to accept it; we want to hold on to something.

Then the next step is the attempt to find a way of occupying ourselves, diverting our attention from our aloneness. The karmic chain reaction begins. Karma is dependent upon the relativity of this and that—my exis tence and my projections—and karma is continually re born as we continually try to busy ourselves. In other words, there is a fear of not being confirmed by our projections. One must constantly try to prove that one does exist by feeling one's projections as a solid thing. Feeling the solidity of something seemingly outside you reassures you that you are a solid entity as well. This is the second skandha, "feeling."

In the third stage, ego develops three strategies or im pulses with which to relate to its projections: indiffer ence, passion and aggression. These impulses are guided by perception. Perception, in this case, is the self-con scious feeling that you must officially report back to central headquarters what is happening in any given moment. Then you can manipulate each situation by organizing another strategy.

In the strategy of indifference, we numb any sensitive areas that we want to avoid, that we think might hurt us. We put on a suit of armor. The second strategy is passion—trying to grasp things and eat them up. It is a magnetizing process. Usually we do not grasp if we feel rich enough. But whenever there is a feeling of poverty, hunger, impotence, then we reach out, we extend our tentacles and attempt to hold onto something. Aggression, the third strategy, is also based upon the experience of poverty, the feeling that you cannot survive and therefore must ward off anything that threatens your property or food. Moreover, the more aware you are of the possibilities of being threatened, the more desperate your reaction becomes. You try to run faster and faster in order to find a way of feeding or defending yourself. This speeding about is a form of aggression. Aggression, passion, indifference are part of the third skandha, "perception/impulse."

Ignorance, feeling, impulse and perception—all are instinctive processes. We operate a radar system which senses our territory. Yet we cannot establish ego properly without intellect, without the ability to conceptualize and name. By now we have an enormously rich collection of things going on inside us. Since we have so many things happening, we begin to categorize them, putting them into certain pigeon-holes, naming them. We make it official, so to speak. So "intellect" or "concept" is the next stage of ego, the fourth skandha, but even this is not quite enough. We need a very active and efficient mechanism to keep the instinctive and intellectual processes of ego coordinated. That is the last development of ego, the fifth skandha, "consciousness."

Consciousness consists of emotions and irregular thought patterns, all of which taken together form the different fantasy worlds with which we occupy ourselves. These fantasy worlds are referred to in the scriptures as the "six realms." The emotions are the highlights of ego, the generals of ego's army; subconscious thought, day-dreams and other thoughts connect one highlight to another. So thoughts form ego's army and are constantly in motion, constantly busy. Our thoughts are neurotic in the sense that they are irregular, changing direction all the time and overlapping one another. We continually jump from one thought to the next, from spiritual thoughts to sexual fantasies to money matters to domestic thoughts and so on. The whole development of the five skandhas—ignorance/form, feeling, impulse/perception, concept and consciousness—is an attempt on our part to shield ourselves from the truth of our insubstantiality.

The practice of meditation is to see the transparency of this shield. But we cannot immediately start dealing with the basic ignorance itself; that would be like trying to push a wall down all at once. If we want to take this wall down, we must take it down brick by brick; we start with immediately available material, a stepping stone. So the practice of meditation starts with the emotions and thoughts, particularly with the thought process.

Self-Absorption

THE SIX REALMS, the different styles of samsaric occupation, are referred to as "realms," in the sense that we dwell within a particular version of reality. We are fascinated with maintaining familiar surroundings, fa-

miliar desires and longings, so as not to give in to a
spacious state of mind. We cling to our habitual patterns
because confusion provides a tremendously familiar
ground to sink into as well as a way of occupying ourselves. We are afraid to give up this security and entertainment, afraid to step into open space, into a meditative state of mind. The prospect of the awakened state
is very irritating because we are uncertain how to handle
it, so we prefer to run back to our prison rather than
release ourselves from it. Confusion and suffering become an occupation, often quite secure and delightful.

The six realms are: the realm of the gods, the realm
of the jealous gods, the human realm, the animal realm,
the realm of the hungry ghosts and the hell realm. The
realms are predominantly emotional attitudes toward
ourselves and our surroundings, emotional attitudes
colored and reinforced by conceptual explanations and
rationalizations. As human beings we may, during the
course of a day, experience the emotions of all of the
realms, from the pride of the god realm to the hatred
and paranoia of the hell realm. Nonetheless, a person's
psychology is usually firmly rooted in one realm. This
realm provides us with a style of confusion, a way of
entertaining and occupying ourselves so as not to have
to face our fundamental uncertainty, our ultimate fear
that we may not exist.

The fundamental occupation of the god realm is
mental fixation, a meditative absorption of sorts, which
is based upon ego, upon the spiritually materialistic
approach. In such meditation practice the meditator
maintains himself by dwelling upon something. The
particular topic of meditation, no matter how seemingly
profound, is experienced as a solid body rather than as

transparent. This practice of meditation begins with a tremendous amount of preparation or "self-development." Actually the aim of such practice is not so much to create the solidity of a place to dwell as it is to create the self-consciousness of the dweller. There is tremendous self-consciousness, which of course reaffirms the meditator's existence.

You do get very dramatic results from such practice, if you are successful at it. One might experience inspiring visions or sounds, seemingly profound mental states, physical bliss and mental bliss. All sorts of "altered states of consciousness" could be experienced or manufactured through the efforts of self-conscious mind. But these experiences are imitations, plastic flowers, manmade, manufactured, prefabricated.

We could dwell on a technique as well—repetition of a *mantra* or visualization. One is not completely absorbed into the visualization or mantra, but instead *you* are visualizing, *you* are repeating the mantra. Such practice, based upon "me," that "I am doing this," is once again the development of self-consciousness.

The realm of the gods is realized through tremendous struggle, is manufactured out of hope and fear. The fear of failure and the hope of gain builds up and up and up to a crescendo. One moment you think you are going to make it and the next moment you think you are going to fail. Alternation between these extremes produces enormous tension. Success and failure mean so much to us—"This is the end of me," or "This is my achievement of ultimate pleasure."

Finally we become so excited that we begin to lose the reference points of our hope and fear. We lose track of where we are and what we were doing. And then

there is a sudden flash in which pain and pleasure become completely one and the meditative state of dwelling
on the ego dawns upon us. Such a breakthrough, such
a tremendous achievement. And then pleasure begins to
saturate our system, psychologically and physically. We
no longer have to care about hope or fear. And quite
possibly we might believe this to be the permanent
achievement of enlightenment or union with God. At
that moment everything we see appears to be beautiful,
loving, even the most grotesque situations of life seem
heavenly. Anything that is unpleasant or aggressive
seems beautiful because we have achieved oneness with
ego. In other words, ego lost track of its intelligence.
This is the absolute, ultimate achievement of bewilderment, the depths of ignorance—extremely powerful. It
is a kind of spiritual atomic bomb, self-destructive in
terms of compassion, in terms of communication, in
terms of stepping out of the bondage of ego. The whole
approach in the realm of the gods is stepping in and in
and in, churning out more and more chains with which
to bind oneself. The more we develop our practice, the
more bondage we create. The scriptures cite the analogy
of the silkworm which binds itself with its own silk
thread until it finally suffocates itself.

Actually we have only been discussing one of two
aspects of the realm of the gods, the self-destructive per-
version of spirituality into materialism. However, the
god realm's version of materialism can also be applied
to so-called worldly concerns in the search for extreme
mental and physical pleasure, the attempt to dwell on
seductive goals of all kinds: health, wealth, beauty, fame,
virtue, whatever. The approach is always pleasure-
oriented, in the sense of maintenance of ego. What char-
acterizes the realm of the gods is the losing track of

hope and fear. And this might be achieved in terms of sensual concerns as well as in terms of spirituality. In both cases, in order to achieve such extraordinary happiness, we must lose track of who is searching and what is the goal. If our ambition expresses itself in terms of worldly pursuits, at first we search for happiness, but then we begin to enjoy the struggle toward happiness as well and we begin to relax into our struggle. Half-way to achieving absolute pleasure and comfort we begin to give in and make the best of our situation. The struggle becomes an adventure and then a vacation or holiday. We are still on our adventurous journey to the actual ultimate goal, but at the same time we consider every step along the way a vacation, a holiday.

So the realm of the gods is not particularly painful, in itself. The pain comes from the eventual disillusionment. You think you have achieved a continually blissful state, spiritual or worldly; you are dwelling on that. But suddenly something shakes you and you realize that what you have achieved is not going to last forever. Your bliss becomes shaky and more irregular, and the thought of maintenance begins to reappear in your mind as you try to push yourself back into your blissful state. But the karmic situation brings you all kinds of irritations and at some stage you begin to lose faith in the continuity of the blissful state. A sudden violence arises, the feeling that you have been cheated, that you cannot stay in this realm of the gods forever. So when the karmic situation shakes you and provides extraordinary situations for you to relate with, the whole process becomes profoundly disappointing. You condemn yourself or the person who put you into the god realm or what brought you out of it. You develop anger and disappointment because you think you have been cheated. You switch into another style of relating to the world, another realm. This is what is called samsara, which literally means "continual circle," "whirlpool," the ocean of confusion which spins around again and again and again, without end.

Paranoia

THE DOMINANT characteristic of the next realm, the jealous god or *asura* realm, is paranoia. If you are trying to help someone who has an asura mentality, they interpret your action as an attempt to oppress them or infiltrate their territory. But if you decide not to help them, they interpret that as a selfish act: you are seeking comfort for yourself. If you present both alternatives to them, then they think you are playing games with them. The asura mentality is quite intelligent: it sees all the hidden corners. You think that you are communicating with an asura face to face, but in actual fact he is looking at you from behind your back. This intense paranoia is combined with an extreme efficiency and accuracy which inspires a defensive form of pride. The asura mentality is associated with wind, speeding about, trying to achieve everything on the spot, avoiding all possibilities of being attacked. It is trying constantly to attain something higher and greater. To do so one must watch out for every possible pitfall. There is no time to prepare, to get ready to put your action into practice. You just act without preparation. A false kind of spontaneity, a sense of freedom to act develops.

The asura mentality is preoccupied with comparison. In the constant struggle to maintain security and achieve greater things, you need points of reference, landmarks to plot your movement, to fix your opponent, to measure your progress. You regard life situations as games, in the sense of there being an opponent and yourself. You are constantly dealing with them and me, me and my friends, me and myself. All corners are regarded as being suspicious or threatening, therefore one must look into them and be careful of them. But one is not careful in the sense of hiding or camouflaging oneself. You are very direct and willing to come out in the open and fight if there is a problem or if there is a plot or a seeming plot against you. You just come out and fight face to face, trying to expose the plot. At the same time that one is going out in the open and facing the situation, one is distrustful of the messages that you receive from the situation, so you ignore them. You refuse to accept any thing, refuse to learn anything that is presented by outsiders, because everyone is regarded as the enemy.

Passion

PASSION IS THE major occupation in the human realm. Passion in this sense is an intelligent kind of grasping in which the logical reasoning mind is always geared toward the creation of happiness. There is an acute sense of the separateness of pleasurable objects from the experiencer resulting in a sense of loss, poverty,

often accompanied by nostalgia. You feel that only pleasurable objects can bring you comfort and happiness,
but you feel inadequate, not strong or magnetic enough
for the objects of pleasure to be drawn naturally into
your territory. Nevertheless, you try actively to draw
them in. This often leads to a critical attitude toward
other people. You want to magnetize the best qualities,
the most pleasurable, most sophisticated, most civilized
situations.

This kind of magnetizing is different from that of the
asura realm which is not as selective and intelligent. The
human realm by comparison involves a high degree of
selectivity and fussiness. There is an acute sense of having your own ideology and your own style, of rejecting
things not your style. You must have the right balance
in everything. You criticize and condemn people who do
not meet your standards. Or else you might be impressed
by someone who embodies your style or is superior to
you at achieving it, someone who is very intelligent and
has very refined taste, who leads a pleasurable life and
has the things you would like to have. It might be an
historical figure or a mythological figure or one of your
contemporaries who has greatly impressed you. He is
very accomplished and you would like to possess his
qualities. It is not simply a matter of being jealous of
another person; you want to draw that person into your
territory. It is an ambitious kind of jealousy in that you
want to equal the other person.

The essence of the human realm is the endeavor to
achieve some high ideal. Often those who find themselves in this realm will have visions of Christ or Buddha
or Krishna or Mohammed or other historical figures who
have tremendous meaning for them because of their
achievements. These great personages have magnetized

everything that one could possibly think of—fame, power,
wisdom. If they wanted to become rich they could do so
because of their enormous influence over other people.
You would like to be like them—not necessarily better
than but at least equal to them. Often people have visions
in which they identify themselves with great politicians,
statesmen, poets, painters, musicians, scientists, and so
forth. There is an heroic attitude, the attempt to create
monuments, the biggest, greatest, historical monument.
This heroic approach is based on fascination with what
you lack. When you hear of someone who possesses re-
markable qualities, you regard them as significant beings
and yourself as insignificant. This continual comparing
and selecting generates a never-ending procession of
desires.

The human mentality places a strong emphasis on
knowledge, learning and education, on collecting all
kinds of information and wisdom. The intellect is most
active in the human realm. There is so much going on
in your mind as a result of having collected so many
things and having planned so many projects. The epitome of the human realm is to be stuck in a huge traffic
jam of discursive thought. You are so busy thinking that
you cannot learn anything at all. The constant churning
out of ideas, plans, hallucinations and dreams is a quite
different mentality from that of the god realm. There
you are completely absorbed in a blissful state, a kind
of self-stuck sense of satisfaction. In the jealous god
realm you are completely drunk on competitiveness;
there is less possibility of thought happening because
your experiences are so strong that they overpower you,
hypnotize you. In the case of the human realm there are
more thoughts happening. The intellectual or logical
mind becomes much more powerful so that one is com-

pletely overwhelmed by the possibilities of magnetizing new situations. Thus one tries to grasp new ideas, new strategies, relevant case histories, quotations from books, significant incidents that have occurred in one's life, and so on, and one's mind becomes completely full of thought. The things that have been recorded in the subconscious play back continually, much more so than in the other realms.

So it is a very intellectual realm, very busy and very disturbing. The human mentality has less pride than the mentalities of the other realms. In the other realms you find some occupation to hang onto and derive satisfaction from, whereas in the human realm there is no such satisfaction. There is a constant searching, constant looking for new situations or attempts to improve given situations. It is the least enjoyable state of mind because suffering is not regarded as an occupation nor as a way of challenging oneself; rather it is a constant reminder of ambitions created out of suffering.

Stupidity

THE DESCRIPTIONS of the different realms are related to subtle but distinct differences in the ways individuals handle themselves in daily life—how they walk, talk, write letters, the way they read, eat, sleep and so on. Everyone tends to develop a style which is peculiar to them. If we hear a tape recording of our voice or see a videotape or movie of ourselves, we are often shocked to see our style as someone else sees it. It feels extremely alien. Usually we find other people's point of view irritating or embarrassing.

Blindness to our style, to how others see us, is most acute in the animal realm. I am not speaking of literally being reborn as an animal but of the animal quality of mind, a mentality which stubbornly pushes forward toward predetermined goals. The animal mentality is very serious. It even makes humor into a serious occupation. Self-consciously trying to create a friendly environment, a person will crack jokes or try to be funny, intimate or clever. However, animals do not really smile or laugh; they just behave. They may play, but it is unusual for animals to actually laugh. They might make friendly noises or gestures, but the subtleties of a sense of humor are absent. The animal mentality looks directly ahead, as if wearing blinders. It never looks to the right or left but very sincerely goes straight ahead, trying to reach the next available situation, continually trying to adjust situations to make them conform to its expectations.

The animal realm is associated with stupidity: that is, preferring to play deaf and dumb, preferring to follow the rules of available games rather than redefine them. Of course, you might try to manipulate your perception of any given game, but you are really just following along, just following your instinct. You have some hidden or secret wish that you would like to put into effect, so when you come to obstacles, to irritations, you just push forward, regardless of whether or not you may hurt someone or destroy something of value. You just go out and pursue whatever is available and if something else comes up, you take advantage of that as well and pursue it.

The ignorance or stupidity of the animal realm comes from a deadly honest and serious mentality which is quite different from the bewilderment of the basic ignorance of the first skandha. In animal ignorance you have a certain style of relating to yourself and refuse to see that style from other points of view. You completely ignore such possibilities. If somebody attacks you or challenges your clumsiness, your unskilled way of handling a situation, you find a way of justifying yourself, find a rationale to keep your self-respect. You are not concerned with being truthful as long as your deception can be maintained in front of others. You are proud that you are clever enough to lie successfully. If you are attacked, challenged, criticized, you automatically find an answer. Such stupidity can be very clever. It is ignorance or stupidity in the sense that you do not see the environment around you, but you see only your goal and only the means to achieve that goal, and you invent all kinds of excuses to prove that you are doing the right thing .

The animal mentality is extremely stubborn, but this stubbornness can be sophisticated as well and quite skillful and ingenious, but without a sense of humor. The ultimate sense of humor is a free way of relating with life situations in their full absurdity. It is seeing things clearly, including self-deception, without blinders, without barriers, without excuses. It is being open and seeing with panoramic vision rather than trying to relieve tension. As long as humor is used as a way to relieve tension or self-consciousness or pressure, then it is the humor of the animal realm, which is actually extremely serious. It is a way of looking for a crutch. So the essence of the animal style is to try to fulfill your desires with extreme honesty, sincerity and seriousness. Traditionally, this direct and mean way of relating with the world is symbolized by the pig. The pig does not look to the right or left but just sniffs along, consuming whatever comes in front of its nose; it goes on and on and on, without any sense of discrimination—a very sincere pig.

Whether we are dealing with simple domestic tasks or highly sophisticated intellectual projects, we can have an animal style. It does not matter whether the pig eats expensive sweets or garbage. What is important is *how* he eats. The extreme animal mentality is trapped in a continual, self-contained, self-justifying round of activity. You are not able to relate with the messages given to you by your environment. You do not see yourself mirrored by others. You may be dealing with very intellectual matters, but the style is animal since there is no sense of humor, no way of surrendering or opening. There is a constant demand to move on from one thing to the next, regardless of failures or obstacles. It is like being a tank that rolls along, crushing everything in its path. It does not matter if you run over people or crash through buildings—you just roll along.

Poverty

IN THE PRETA or hungry ghost realm one is preoccupied with the process of expanding, becoming rich, consuming. Fundamentally, you feel poor. You are unable to keep up the pretense of being what you would like to be. Whatever you have is used as proof of the validity of your pride, but it is never enough, there is always some sense of inadequacy.

The poverty mentality is traditionally symbolized by a hungry ghost who has a tiny mouth, the size of the eye of a needle, a thin neck and throat, skinny arms and legs and a gigantic belly. His mouth and neck are too small to let enough food pass through them to fill his immense belly, so he is always hungry. And the struggle to satisfy his hunger is very painful since it is so hard to swallow what he eats. Food, of course, symbolizes anything you may want—friendship, wealth, clothes, sex, power, whatever.

Anything that appears in your life you regard as something to consume. If you see a beautiful autumn leaf falling, you regard it as your prey. You take it home or photograph it or paint a picture of it or write in your memoirs how beautiful it was. If you buy a bottle of Coke, it is exciting to hear the rattlings of the paper bag as you unpack it. The sound of the Coke spilling out of the bottle gives a delightful sense of thirst. Then you self-consciously taste it and swallow it. You have finally managed to consume it—such an achievement. It was fantastic; you brought the dream into reality. But after a while you become restless again and look for something else to consume.

You are constantly hungering for new entertainment —spiritual, intellectual, sensual and so on. Intellectually you may feel inadequate and decide to pull up your socks by studying and listening to juicy, thoughtful answers, profound, mystical words. You consume one idea after another, trying to record them, trying to make them solid and real. Whenever you feel hunger, you open your notebook or scrapbook or a book of satisfying ideas. When you experience boredom or insomnia or depression, you open your books, read your notes and clippings and ponder over them, draw comfort from them. But this becomes repetitive at some point. You would like to re-meet your teachers or find new ones. And another journey to the restaurant or the supermarket or the delicatessen is not a bad idea. But sometimes you are prevented from taking the trip. You may not have enough money, your child gets sick, your parents are dying, you have business to attend to and so on. You realize that when more obstacles come up, then that much more hunger arises in you. And the more you want, the more you realize what you cannot get, which is painful.

It is painful to be suspended in unfulfilled desire, continually searching for satisfaction. But even if you achieve your goal then there is the frustration of becoming stuffed, so full that one is insensitive to further stimuli. You try to hold on to your possession, to dwell on it, but after a while you become heavy and dumb, unable to appreciate anything. You wish you could be hungry again so you could fill yourself up again. Whether you satisfy a desire or suspend yourself in desire and continue to struggle, in either case you are inviting frustration.

Anger

THE HELL REALM is pervaded by aggression. This aggression is based on such a perpetual condition of hatred that one begins to lose track of whom you are building your aggression toward as well as who is being aggressive toward you. There is a continual uncertainty and confusion. You have built up a whole environment of aggression to such a point that finally, even if you were to feel slightly cooler about your own anger and aggression, the environment around you would throw more aggression at you. It is like walking in hot weather: you might feel physically cooler for a while, but hot air is coming at you constantly so you cannot keep yourself cool for long.

The aggression of the hell realm does not seem to be your aggression, but it seems to permeate the whole space around you. There is a feeling of extreme stuffiness and claustrophobia. There is no space in which to breathe, no space in which to act, and life becomes overwhelming. The aggression is so intense that, if you were to kill someone to satisfy your aggression, you would achieve only a small degree of satisfaction. The aggression still lingers around you. Even if you were to try to kill yourself, you would find that the killer remains; so you would not have managed to murder yourself completely. There is a constant environment of aggression in which one never knows who is killing whom. It is like trying to eat yourself from the inside out. Having eaten yourself, the eater remains, and he must be eaten as well, and so on and so on. Each time the crocodile bites his own tail, he is nourished by it; the more he eats, the more he grows. There is no end to it.

You cannot really eliminate pain through aggression. The more you kill, the more you strengthen the killer who will create new things to be killed. The aggression grows until finally there is no space: the whole environment has been solidified. There are not even gaps in which to look back or do a double-take. The whole space has become completely filled with aggression. It is outrageous. There is no opportunity to create a watcher to testify to your destruction, no one to give you a report. But at the same time the aggression grows. The more you destroy, the more you create.

Traditionally aggression is symbolized by the sky and earth radiating red fire. The earth turns into a red hot iron and space becomes an environment of flame and fire. There is no space to breathe any cool air or feel coldness. Whatever you see around you is hot, intense, extremely claustrophobic. The more you try to destroy your enemies or win over your opponents, the more you generate resistence, counter-aggression bouncing back at you.

In the hell realm we throw out flames and radiations which are continually coming back to us. There is no room at all in which to experience any spaciousness or openness. Rather there is a constant effort, which can be very cunning, to close up all the space. The hell realm can only be created through your relationships with the outside world, whereas in the jealous god realm your own psychological hang-ups could be the material for creating the asura mentality. In the hell realm there is a constant situation of relationship; you are trying to play games with something and the attempt bounces back on you, constantly recreating extremely claustrophobic situations; so that finally there is no room in which to communicate at all.

At that point the only way to communicate is by trying to recreate your anger. You thought you had managed to win a war of one-upsmanship, but finally you did not get a response from the other person; you one-upped him right out of existence. So you are faced only with your own aggression coming back at you and it manages to fill up all the space. One is left lonely once more, without excitement, so you seek another way of playing the game, again and again and again. You do not play for enjoyment, but because you do not feel protected nor secure enough. If you have no way to secure yourself, you feel bleak and cold, so you must rekindle the fire. In order to rekindle the fire you have to fight constantly to maintain yourself. One cannot help playing the game; one just finds oneself playing it, all the time.

III
Sitting
Meditation

The Fool

HAVING UNDERSTOOD about ego and neurosis, knowing the situation with which we are confronted, what do we do now? We have to relate with our mental gossip and our emotions simply and directly, without philosophy. We have to use the existing material, which is ego's hang-ups and credentials and deceptions, as a starting point. Then we begin to realize that in order to do this we must actually use some kind of feeble credentials. Token credentials are necessary. Without them we cannot begin. So we practice meditation using simple techniques; the breath is our feeble credential. It is ironic: we were studying buddha-dharma without credentials and now we find ourselves doing something fishy. We are doing the same thing we were criticizing. We feel uncomfortable and embarrassed about the whole thing. Is this another way to charlatanism, another egohood? Is this the same game? Is this teaching trying to make great fun of me, make me look stupid? We are very suspicious. That is fine. It is a sign that our intelligence is sharper. It is a good way to begin, but, nevertheless, finally, we have to do something. We must humble ourselves and acknowledge that despite our intellectual sophistication, our actual awareness of

mind is primitive. We are on the kindergarten level, we
do not know how to count to ten. So by sitting and meditating we acknowledge that we are fools, which is an
extraordinarily powerful and necessary measure. We begin as fools. We sit and meditate. Once we begin to
realize that we are actually one-hundred-percent fools
for doing such a thing, then we begin to see how the
techniques function as a crutch. We do not hang on to
our crutch or regard it as having important mystical
meaning. It is simply a tool which we use as long as we
need it and then put aside.

We must be willing to be completely ordinary people,
which means accepting ourselves as we are without trying to become greater, purer, more spiritual, more in-
sightful. If we can accept our imperfections as they are,
quite ordinarily, then we can use them as part of the
path. But if we try to get rid of our imperfections, then
they will be enemies, obstacles on the road to our "self-
improvement." And the same is true for the breath. If
we can see it as it is, without trying to use it to improve
ourselves, then it becomes a part of the path because
we are no longer using it as the tool of our personal
ambition.

Simplicity

MEDITATION PRACTICE is based on dropping
dualistic fixation, dropping the struggle of good against

bad. The attitude you bring to spirituality should be natural, ordinary, without ambition. Even if you are building good karma, you are still sowing further seeds of karma. So the point is to transcend the karmic process altogether. Transcend both good and bad karma.

There are many references in the tantric literature to *mahasukha,* the great joy, but the reason it is referred to as the great joy is because it transcends both hope and fear, pain and pleasure. Joy here is not pleasurable in the ordinary sense, but it is an ultimate and fundamental sense of freedom, a sense of humor, the ability to see the ironical aspect of the game of ego, the playing of polarities. If one is able to see ego from an aerial point of view, then one is able to see its humorous quality. Therefore the attitude one brings to meditation practice should be very simple, not based upon trying to collect pleasure or avoid pain. Rather meditation is a natural process, working on the material of pain and pleasure as the path.

You do not try to use meditation techniques—prayer, mantra, visualization, rituals, breathing techniques—to create pleasure or to confirm your existence. You do not try to separate yourself from the technique, but you try to become the technique so that there is a sense of nonduality. Technique is a way of imitating the style of non-duality. In the beginning a person uses technique as a kind of game because he is still imagining that he is meditating. But the techniques—physical feeling, sensations and breathing, for instance—are very earthy and tend to ground a person. And the proper attitude toward technique is not to regard it as magical, a miracle or profound ceremony of some kind, but just see it as a simple process, extremely simple. The simpler the technique,

the less the danger of sidetracks because you are not
feeding yourself with all sorts of fascinating, seductive
hopes and fears.

In the beginning the practice of meditation is just
dealing with the basic neurosis of mind, the confused
relationship between yourself and projections, your relationship to thoughts. When a person is able to see the
simplicity of the technique without any special attitude
toward it, then he is able to relate himself with his
thought pattern as well. He begins to see thoughts as
simple phenomena, no matter whether they are pious
thoughts or evil thoughts, domestic thoughts, whatever
they may be. One does not relate to them as belonging
to a particular category, as being good or bad; just see
them as simple thoughts. When you relate to thoughts
obsessively, then you are actually feeding them because
thoughts need your attention to survive. Once you begin to pay attention to them and categorize them, then
they become very powerful. You are feeding them energy
because you have not seen them as simple phenomena.
If one tries to quiet them down, that is another way of
feeding them. So meditation in the beginning is not an
attempt to achieve happiness, nor is it the attempt to
achieve mental calm or peace, though they could be by-
products of meditation. Meditation should not be regarded as a vacation from irritation.

In fact, a person always finds when he begins to practice meditation that all sorts of problems are brought
out. Any hidden aspects of your personality are brought
out into the open, for the simple reason that for the first
time you are allowing yourself to see your state of mind
as it is. For the first time you are not evaluating your
thoughts.

One begins to appreciate more and more the beauty of simplicity. You actually do things for the first time *completely*. Just breathing or walking or whatever the technique may be, you just start doing it and working along with it very simply. Complications become transparent complications rather than solidified ones. So the first step in dealing with ego is to begin with a very simple way of dealing with thoughts. Not dealing with them in the sense of quieting them down, but just see their transparent quality.

Sitting meditation needs to be combined with an awareness practice in everyday life. In awareness practice you begin to feel the after-effects of sitting meditation. Your simple relationship with breathing and your simple relationship with thoughts continues. And every situation of life becomes a simple relationship—a simple relationship with the kitchen sink, a simple relationship with your car, a simple relationship with your father, mother, children. Of course this is not to say that a person suddenly is transformed into a saint. Familiar irritations are still there of course, but they are simple irritations, transparent irritations.

Little domestic things may not seem to be important or meaningful, but dealing with them in a very simple way is extremely valuable and helpful. If a person is able to perceive the simplicity as it is, then meditation becomes 24-hour-a-day work. One begins to experience a tremendous sense of space because one does not have to watch oneself in a very heavy-handed way. Rather you are the recipient of the situation. Of course you may still comment upon and watch this process, but when you sit in meditation you just are; you do not use the breath or any other techniques. You are getting into the grip of something. Finally you do not need a translator any more, a watcher any more. Then the language is understood properly.

Mindfulness and Awareness

MEDITATION IS WORKING with our speed, our restlessness, our constant busyness. Meditation provides space or ground in which restlessness might function, might have room to be restless, might relax by being restless. If we do not interfere with restlessness, then restlessness becomes part of the space. We do not control or attack the desire to catch our next tail.

Meditation practice is not a matter of trying to produce a hypnotic state of mind or create a sense of restfulness. Trying to achieve a restful state of mind reflects a mentality of poverty. Seeking a restful state of mind, one is on guard against restlessness. There is a constant sense of paranoia and limitation. We feel a need to be on guard against the sudden fits of passion or aggression which might take us over, make us lose control. This guarding process limits the scope of the mind by not accepting whatever comes.

Instead, meditation should reflect a mentality of richness in the sense of using everything that occurs in the state of mind. Thus, if we provide enough room for restlessness so that it might function within the space, then the energy ceases to be restless because it can trust itself fundamentally. Meditation is giving a huge, luscious meadow to a restless cow. The cow might be restless for a while in its huge meadow, but at some stage, because there is so much space, the restlessness becomes irrelevant. So the cow eats and eats and eats and relaxes and falls asleep.

Acknowledging restlessness, identifying with it, requires mindfulness, whereas providing a luscious meadow, a big space for the restless cow requires awareness. So mindfulness and awareness always complement each other. Mindfulness is the process of relating with individual situations directly, precisely, definitely. You communicate or connect with problematic situations or irritating situations in a simple way. There is ignorance, there is restlessness, there is passion, there is aggression. They need not be praised or condemned. They are just regarded as fits. They are conditioned situations, but they could be seen accurately and precisely by the unconditioned mindfulness. Mindfulness is like a microscope; it is neither an offensive nor a defensive weapon in relation to the germs we observe through it. The function of the microscope is just to clearly present what is there. Mindfulness need not refer to the past or the future; it is fully in the now. At the same time it is an active mind involved in dualistic perceptions, for it is necessary in the beginning to use that kind of discriminating judgment.

Awareness is seeing the discovery of mindfulness. We do not have to dispose of or keep the contents of mind. The precision of mindfulness could be left as it is because it has its own environment, its own space. We do not have to make decisions to throw it away or keep it as a treasure. Thus awareness is another step toward

choicelessness in situations. The Sanskrit word for awareness is *smriti* which means "recognition," "recollection."
Recollection not in the sense of remembering the past
but in the sense of recognizing the product of mindfulness. The mindfulness provides some ground, some room
for recognition of aggression, passion and so on. Mindfulness provides the topic or the terms or the words, and
awareness is the grammar which goes around and correctly locates the terms. Having experienced the precision of mindfulness, we might ask the question of
ourselves, "What should I do with that? What can I do
next?" And awareness reassures us that we do not really
have to do anything with it but can leave it in its own
natural place. It is like discovering a beautiful flower in
the jungle; shall we pick the flower and bring it home or
shall we let the flower stay in the jungle? Awareness says
leave the flower in the jungle, since it is the natural place
for that plant to grow. So awareness is the willingness
not to cling to the discoveries of mindfulness, and mindfulness is just precision; things are what they are. Mindfulness is the vanguard of awareness. We flash on a
situation and then diffuse that one-pointedness into
awareness.

So mindfulness and awareness work together to bring
acceptance of living situations as they are. We need not
regard life as worth boycotting or indulging in. Life
situations are the food of awareness and mindfulness;
we cannot meditate without the depressions and excitement that go on in life. We wear out the shoe of samsara
by walking on it through the practice of meditation. The
combination of mindfulness and awareness maintains
the journey, so meditation practice or spiritual development depends upon samsara. From the aerial point of

view, we could say that there need not be samsara or nirvana, that making the journey is useless. But since we are on the ground, making the journey is extraordinarily useful.

Boredom

WE MUST USE the human body as an analogy to describe the development of ego. In this analogy, the fundamental dualism, feeling, impulse and concepts are like the bones of the body. Emotions are like the muscles of the body and subconscious gossip and all the little mental activities are the circulatory system which feeds and sustains the muscles. So in order to have a completely functioning body we need to have a muscle system and a circulatory system and bones to support them.

We begin meditation practice by dealing with thoughts, the fringe of ego. The practice of meditation is an undoing process. If you want to dissect and examine the body of ego, you start by cutting a slit in the skin and then you cut through the arteries. So the practitioner who is not involved with credentials begins with an operation. Credentials are an illness and you need an operation to remove them. With your sickness you are trying to prove that you exist. "I am sick, therefore I am real, I feel pain." So the operation is to eliminate the notion of being an important person simply because you are sick. Of course you can attract all kinds of atten-

tion if you declare that you are sick. Then you can phone
your relatives and friends and tell them that you are
sick and they will come and help you.

That is a very wretched way of proving your existence.
That is precisely what the credentials do. They prove
that you are sick so that you can have attention from
your friends. We have to operate on this person to eliminate the credential sickness. But if we give this person
an anesthetic, he will not realize how much he has to
give up. So we should not use anesthetics at all. It should
be like natural childbirth. The mother sees her child
being born, how it comes out of her body, how it enters
into the outside world. Giving birth to buddha-dharma
without credentials should be the same; you should see
the whole process. You are taken straight to the operating room. Now, in the operating theater, the first step
of the operation is to make a little slit in the area of
complaint with an extraordinarily sharp surgical knife,
the sword of Manjushri, the sword of compassion and
wisdom. Just a little slit is made, which is not as painful
as we expected.

Sitting and meditating is the little slit in your artery.
You may have been told that sitting meditation is extremely boring and difficult to accomplish. But you do
not find it all that difficult. In fact it seems quite easy.
You just sit. The artery, which is the subconscious gossip
in your mind, is cut through by using certain techniques
—either working on breathing or walking or whatever.
It is a very humble gesture on your part—just sit and
cut through your thoughts, just welcome your breathing
going out and in, just natural breathing, no special
breathing, just sit and develop the watchfulness of your
breathing. It is not concentrating on breathing. Concen-

tration involves something to grasp, something to hold on to. You are "here" trying to concentrate on something "there." Rather than concentration we practice mindfulness. We see what is happening there rather than developing concentration, which is goal-oriented. Anything connected with goals involves a journey toward somewhere from somewhere. In mindfulness practice there is no goal, no journey; you are just mindful of what is happening there.

There is no promise of love and light or visions of any kind—no angels, no devils. Nothing happens: it is absolutely boring. Sometimes you feel silly. One often asks the question, "Who is kidding whom? Am I on to something or not?" You are not on to something. Travelling the path means you get off everything, there is no place to perch. Sit and feel your breath, be with it. Then you begin to realize that actually the slitting of the artery did not take place when you were introduced to the practice. The actual slitting takes place when you begin to feel the boredom of the practice—real boredom. "I'm supposed to get something out of Buddhism and meditation. I'm supposed to attain different levels of realization. I haven't. I'm bored stiff." Even your watcher is unsympathetic to you, begins to mock you. Boredom is important because boredom is anti-credential. Credentials are entertaining, always bringing you something new, something lively, something fantastic, all kinds of solutions. When you take away the idea of credentials, then there is boredom.

We had a film workshop in Colorado in which we discussed whether it was important to entertain people or make a good film. And what I said was that perhaps the audience might be bored with what we have to pre-

sent, but we must raise the intelligence, the standards
of the audience, up to the level of what we are presenting, rather than trying to constantly match their expectations, their desire for entertainment. Once you begin to
try to satisfy the audience's desire for entertainment, you
constantly bend down and bend down and bend down,
until the whole thing becomes absurd. If a film-maker
presents his own ideas with dignity, his work might be
ill-received in the beginning but possibly well-received
once people begin to catch up to it. The film might raise
the audience's level of sophistication.

Similarly, boredom is important in meditation practice; it increases the psychological sophistication of the
practitioners. They begin to appreciate boredom and they
develop their sophistication until the boredom begins to
become cool boredom, like a mountain river. It flows
and flows and flows, methodically and repetitiously, but
it is very cooling, very refreshing. Mountains never get
tired of being mountains and waterfalls never get tired
of being waterfalls. Because of their patience we begin
to appreciate them. There is something in that. I don't
want to sound especially romantic about the whole thing,
I am trying to paint a black picture, but I slipped a bit.
It is a good feeling to be bored, constantly sitting and
sitting. First gong, second gong, third gong, more gongs
yet to come. Sit, sit, sit, sit. Cut through the artery until
the boredom becomes extraordinarily powerful. We have
to work hard at it.

At this point we cannot really study the vajrayana or,
for that matter, even the mahayana. We are not up to it
because we have not actually made a relationship with
boredom yet. To begin with we have to relate with the
hinayana. If we are to save ourselves from spiritual ma-

terialism and from buddha-dharma with credentials, if we are to become the dharma without credentials, the introduction of boredom and repetitiousness is extremely important. Without it we have no hope. It is true—no hope.

There are definite styles of boredom. The Zen tradition in Japan creates a definite style of boredom in its monasteries. Sit, cook, eat. Sit zazen and do your walking meditation and so on. But to an American novice who goes to Japan or takes part in traditional Japanese practice in this country, the message of boredom is not communicated properly. Instead, if I may say so, it turns into a militant appreciation of rigidity, or an aesthetic appreciation of simplicity, rather than actually being bored, which is strange. Actually it was not designed to be that way. To the Japanese, Zen practice is an ordinary Japanese life-situation in which you just do your daily work and sit a lot of zazen. But Americans appreciate the little details—how you use your bowl and how you eat consciously in zazen posture. This is only supposed to create a feeling of boredom, but to American students it is a work of art. Cleaning your bowl, washing it out, folding your white napkin and so forth, becomes living theater. The black cushion is supposed to suggest no color, complete boredom. But for Americans it inspires a mentality of militant blackness, straightforwardness.

The tradition is trying to bring out boredom, which is a necessary aspect of the narrow path of discipline, but instead the practice turns out to be an archeological, sociological survey of interesting things to do, something you could tell your friends about: "Last year I spent the whole fall sitting in a Zen monastery for six months. I watched autumn turn into winter and I did my zazen practice and everything was so precise and beautiful. I learned how to sit and I even learned how to walk and eat. It was a wonderful experience and I did not get bored at all."

You tell your friends, "Go, it's great fun," and you collect another credential. The attempt to destroy credentials creates another credential. The first point in destroying ego's game is the strict discipline of sitting meditation practice. No intellectual speculation, no philosophizing. Just sit and do it. That is the first strategy in developing buddha-dharma without credentials.

The Way of the Buddha

BOREDOM HAS MANY aspects: there is the sense that nothing is happening, that something might happen, or even that what we would like to happen might replace that which is not happening. Or, one might appreciate boredom as a delight. The practice of meditation could be described as relating with cool boredom, refreshing boredom, boredom like a mountain stream. It refreshes because we do not have to do anything or expect anything. But there must be some sense of discipline if we are to get beyond the frivolity of trying to replace boredom. That is why we work with the breath as our practice of meditation. Simply relating with the breath is very monotonous and unadventurous—we do not discover that the third eye is opening or that *cakras* are unfolding. It is like a stone-carved Buddha sitting in the desert. Nothing, absolutely nothing, happens.

As we realize that nothing is happening, strangely we begin to realize that something dignified is happening. There is no room for frivolity, no room for speed. We just breathe and are there. There is something very satisfying and wholesome about it. It is as though we had eaten a good meal and were satisfied with it, in contrast to eating and trying to satisfy oneself. It is a very simple-minded approach to sanity.

It is recorded that the Buddha was given many Hindu meditation practices. He scorched himself in fires. He related with the energy of tantra by visualizing all kinds of things. He saw a neurological light by pressing his eyeballs and he heard a neurological buzz of supposedly yogic sound by pressing his ears. He went through all of this himself and realized that these phenomena were gimmicks rather than real *samadhi* or meditation. Maybe the Buddha was a dumb yoga student without any imagination. However, we follow his dumbness, his example as the enlightened one, the *samyaksambuddha,* the completely enlightened one.

As the Buddha's approach to the practice of meditation evolved, he realized that gimmicks are merely neurotic affectations. He decided to look for what is simple, what is actually there, to discover the relationship between mind and body, his relationship with the kusha grass mat on which he sat and the *bodhi* tree above his head. He looked into his relationships with everything very simply and directly. It was not especially exciting—there were no flashes of anything—but it was reassuring. At the dawn of his enlightenment someone asked the Buddha, "What are your credentials? How do we know

that you are enlightened?" He touched his hand to the
ground. "This solid earth is my witness. This solid earth,
this same earth, is my witness." Sane and solid and definite, no imaginings, no concepts, no emotions, no frivolity, but being basically what is: this is the awakened
state. And this is the example we follow in our meditation practice.

As far as Buddha was concerned, at that point it was
not the message but the implications that were more important. And, as followers of Buddha, we have this approach, which is the idea of *vipashyana,* literally meaning
"insight." Insight is relating not only with what you see
but also with the implications of it, the totality of the
space and objects around it. Breath is the object of meditation, but the environment around the breath is also
part of the meditative situation.

The Buddha then turned the wheel of the dharma,
expounding the four noble truths: pain, the origin of
pain, the goal and the path. All this was inspired by his
discovery that there is tremendous space in which the
universality of inspiration is happening. There is pain,
but there is also the environment around the origin of
pain. The whole thing becomes more expansive, more
open. He wasn't such a bad yoga student after all. Quite
possibly he was not good at *hatha yoga,* but he saw the
environment around hatha yoga and *pranayama.*

The Buddha's demonstrations of basic sanity were
spontaneous. He did not preach or teach in the ordinary
sense but, as he unfolded, the energy of compassion and
the endless resources of generosity developed within him
and people began to find this out. That kind of activity
of the Buddha is the vipashyana practice that we are
attempting. It is realizing that space contains matter,

that matter makes no demands on space and that space makes no demands on matter. It is a reciprocal and open situation. Everything is based on compassion and openness. Compassion is not particularly emotional in the sense that you feel bad that someone is suffering, that you are better than others and that you have to help them. Compassion is that total openness in which the Buddha had no ground, no sense of territory. So much so, that he was hardly an individual. He was just a grain of sand living in the vast desert. Through his insignificance he became the "world enlightened one," because there was no battle involved. The dharma he taught was passionless, without aggression. Passion is grasping, holding on to your territory.

So our practice of meditation, if we follow the Buddha's way, is the practice of passionlessness or nonaggression. It is dealing with the possessiveness of aggression: "This is my spiritual trip and I don't want you to interfere with it. Get out of my territory." Spirituality, or the vipashyana perspective, is a panoramic situation in which you can come and go freely and your relationship with the world is open. It is the ultimate nonviolence.

IV
Working with the
Emotions

The Dualistic Barrier

As WE HAVE discussed, boredom is very important in the practice of sitting meditation; there is no other way to reach the depths of meditation practice except through boredom. But at the same time, we must look further at the desire for credentials. Even experiencing boredom or relating with boredom could itself be another game, another way of creating a sense of comfort, a sense of security in the practice of meditation. Something else must be dealt with in addition to experiencing boredom, and this something else is the daily living situation involving love and hate, depression and so forth, the subtle but fundamental emotions.

Although we may be able to accomplish smoothly the vipashyana practice of relating with the breathing, still we cannot ignore this large area of potential and unexpected disturbances. You may finish an ideal sitting meditation period in which you experienced boredom, and then you go out into the living room and decide to make a call to your friend and realize that you haven't paid your telephone bill and the telephone is disconnected. And you get outraged: "But that's not my fault, my wife misplaced the bill," or "They have no right to do this," or whatever.

Little things like that happen all the time. If we experience such situations, then we begin to realize that our practice is credential-oriented, that there is a belief in some kind of basic harmony. The problems of everyday life are a way of destroying our credentials, our comfort and security, and they present us with an opportunity to relate with our emotions.

Although we may be able to see the simplicity of the discursive thought process, still there are very strong emotions with which it is extremely difficult and quite challenging to work. In working with the emotions we are dealing not only with the fifth skandha, "consciousness," but also with the fourth skandha, "concept," "intellect." The emotions are composed of energy, which can be likened to water, and a dualistic thought process, which could be likened to pigment or paint. When energy and thought are mixed together they become the vivid and colorful emotions. Concept gives the energy a particular location, a sense of relationship, which makes the emotions vivid and strong. Fundamentally, the reason why emotions are discomforting, painful, frustrating, is because our relationship to the emotions is not quite clear.

At the level of the fifth skandha the structure of ego has become so efficient that there is a conflict between the administration of ego and the central ignorance itself. It is as if the king's minister had become more powerful than the king himself. This seems to be the point where emotions become painful, because you are not quite certain what your relationship to your emotions is. There is tremendous conflict, a feeling that you are being overpowered by your emotions, that you are losing your basic identity, your center of command.

So the pain of emotion comes from this conflict; the relationship is always ambivalent. However, if a person is actually able to relate fully and thoroughly with the emotions, then they cease to become an external problem. One is able to make very close contact with the emotions and the war between your emotions and yourself; you and your projections, you and the world outside, becomes transparent. This involves removing the dualistic barriers set up by concepts, which is the experience of shunyata, the absence of relative concepts, emptiness.

Actually, we do not see things completely as they are. Generally we perceive something, and then we look. Looking in this case is the act of imposing names and associations on things. Seeing things means accepting what they are, but looking means unnecessary effort to make sure that you are safe, that nothing is going to confuse you in your relationship to the world. So we create our security by putting things into categories, naming them, by using relative terms to identify their inter-relationships, how they fit together. And this security brings temporary happiness and comfort.

This very crude way of finding landmarks in terms of our projections is very childish, and one has to repeat the same game again and again. There is no attempt to deal with projections as exciting and fluid situations at all; instead the world is seen as being absolutely solid and stiff. Everything is frozen movement, frozen space, solidified. We see the world as having an extremely hard facade, a metallic or plastic quality. We see the colors as they are, but somehow they are plastic colors rather than rainbow colors. And this solid quality is the dualistic barrier that we have been talking about. Which is not to say that a person should not feel the texture of a stone or a brick as solid. The physical situation of solidity has no relation to psychological solidity. We are dealing here with mental solidity—harshness, a metallic quality. Actually, it is extremely interesting that we see only our own solid version of the world. So perception is very much individualized, centralized on self-consciousness.

It is impossible immediately to experience shunyata— that is, absence of concept, absence of the dualistic barrier. We must start with a simple practice in the beginning, and then we begin to perceive the transparent quality of thoughts and emotions. Then we must also try to step beyond the relational situation of transparency— that is, the sense of "you" seeing the transparency of thoughts and emotions. In other words, the thought process and the emotions are transparent and they are taking place in the midst of nowhere, in space. That spacious quality, when everything operates and occurs in space, is the positive space of skillful means, of working with everyday life-situations. In fact, the creativity and the positive aspect of the emotions and life-situations can only be seen through experiencing the space rather than the product. If a person's relationship to space is developed properly, perceived properly, then there is no hesitation at all.

We are speaking here of becoming *one* with the emotions. This is different from and in contrast to the usual approach of suppressing them or acting them out. If we are suppressing our emotions, it is extremely dangerous because we are regarding them as something terrible, shameful, which means that our relationship to our emotions is not really open. Once we try to suppress them, sooner or later they are going to step out and explode.

There is another possibility. If you do not suppress your emotions, then you really allow yourself to come out and be carried away by them. This way of dealing with the emotions also comes from a kind of panic; your relationship with your emotions has not been properly reconciled. This is another way of escaping from the actual emotion, another kind of release, a false release. It is a confusion of mind and matter, thinking that the physical act of practicing emotions, of putting them into effect, supposedly will cure the emotions, relieve their irritation. But generally it reinforces them, and the emotions become more powerful. The relationship between the emotions and mind is not quite clear here.

So the intelligent way of working with emotions is to try to relate with their basic substance, the abstract quality of the emotions, so to speak. The basic "isness" quality of the emotions, the fundamental nature of the emotions, is just energy. And if one is able to relate with energy, then the energies have no conflict with you. They become a natural process. So trying to suppress or getting carried away by the emotions become irrelevant once a person is completely able to see their basic characteristic, the emotions as they are, which is shunyata. The barrier, the wall between you and your projections, the hysterical and paranoid aspect of your relationship to your projections, has been removed—not exactly removed, but seen through. When there is no panic involved in dealing with the emotions, then you can deal with them completely, properly. Then you are like someone who is completely skilled in his profession, who does not panic, but just does his work completely, thoroughly.

We have been discussing how to deal with consciousness, the last stage of the development of ego, and we have also dealt with the prior stage of concept. When we speak of "dealing" with them, it is not a question of eliminating them completely but of really seeing them and transmuting their confused qualities into transcendental qualities. We still use the energies of thought, the energies of the emotions and the energies of concept. Generally, when the idea of ego is presented, the immediate reaction on the part of the audience is to regard it as a villain, an enemy. You feel you must destroy this ego, this me, which is a masochistic and suicidal approach. People tend to think this way because, usually when we speak of spirituality, we tend to think that we are fighting the bad; we are good, spirituality is the ultimate good, the epitome of good, and the other side is bad. But true spirituality is not a battle; it is the ultimate practice of non-violence. We are not regarding any part of us as being a villain, an enemy, but we are trying to use everything as a part of the natural process of life. As soon as a notion of polarity between good and bad develops, then we are caught in spiritual materialism, which is working to achieve happiness in a simple-minded sense, on the way to egohood. So the dualistic wall is not something we have to destroy or eliminate or exorcise. But having seen the emotions as they are, we have more material with which to work creatively. This makes it quite clear that the notion of samsara is dependent upon the notion of nirvana, and the notion of nirvana is dependent upon the notion of samsara; they are interdependent. If there were no confusion, there would be no wisdom.

Lion's Roar

THE "LION'S ROAR" is the fearless proclamation
that any state of mind, including the emotions, is a workable situation, a reminder in the practice of meditation.
We realize that chaotic situations must not be rejected.
Nor must we regard them as regressive, as a return to confusion. We must respect whatever happens to our state of
mind. Chaos should be regarded as extremely good news.

There are several stages in relating with the emotions;
the stages of seeing, hearing, smelling, touching and
transmuting. In the case of seeing the emotions, we have
a general awareness that the emotions have their own
space, their own development. We accept them as part
of the pattern of mind, without question, without reference back to the scriptures, without help from credentials, but we directly acknowledge that they are so, that
these things are happening. And then hearing involves
experiencing the pulsation of such energy, the energy
upsurge as it comes toward you. Smelling is appreciating
that the energy is somewhat workable, as when you smell
food and the smell becomes an appetizer, whetting your
appetite before you eat. It smells like a good meal, it
smells delicious, although you have not eaten it yet. It
is somewhat workable. Touching is feeling the nitty-
gritty of the whole thing, that you can touch and relate

with it, that your emotions are not particularly destructive or crazy but just an upsurge of energy, whatever form they take—aggressive, passive or grasping. Transmutation is not a matter of rejecting the basic qualities of the emotions. Rather, as in the alchemical practice of changing lead into gold, you do not reject the basic qualities of the material, but you change its appearance and substance somewhat. So you experience emotional upheaval as it is but still work with it, become one with it. The usual problem is that, when emotions arise, we feel that we are being challenged by them, that they will overwhelm our self-existence or the credentials of our existence. However, if we become the embodiment of hatred or passion, then we do not have any personal credentials any more. Usually that is why we react against the emotions, because we feel we might be taken over by them, that we might freak out, lose our heads. We are afraid that aggression or depression will become so overwhelming that we will lose our ability to function normally, that we will forget how to brush our teeth, how to dial a telephone.

There is a fear that emotion might become too much, that we might fall into it and lose our dignity, our role as human beings. Transmutation involves going through such fear. Let yourself be in the emotion, go through it, give in to it, experience it. You begin to go toward the emotion, rather than just experiencing the emotion coming toward you. A relationship, a dance, begins to develop. Then the most powerful energies become absolutely workable rather than taking you over, because there is nothing to take over if you are not putting up any resistance. Whenever there is no resistance, a sense of rhythm occurs. The music and the dance take place at the same time. That is the lion's roar. Whatever occurs in the samsaric mind is regarded as the path; everything is workable. It is a fearless proclamation—the lion's roar. As long as we create "patches" to cover what we regard as unworkable situations—metaphysical, philosophical, religious patches—then our action is not the lion's roar. It is a coward's scream—very pathetic.

Usually, whenever we feel that we cannot work with something, automatically we look back and try to find some external resource, some patch to conceal our insufficiency. Our concern is to save face, avoid being embarrassed, avoid being challenged by our emotions. How might we put another patch on top of another patch in order to get out of this situation? We could burden ourselves with millions upon millions of patches, one on top of the other. If the first one is too delicate, then the second may be stronger, so we end up creating a suit of patches, a suit of armor. But here we have some problems. The joints in our armor begin to squeak and there are holes in the armor where the joints are. It is difficult to put patches on the joints, because we still want to move, still want to dance, but we do not want to squeak. We want to have joints in order to move. So unless one is completely mummified, which is death, being a corpse, there is no way to completely protect oneself. For a living human being patchwork is an absolutely impractical idea.

So the buddha-dharma without credentials is, from this point of view, the same thing as the lion's roar. We do not need patches any more. We could transmute the substance of the emotions, which is an extremely powerful act. Indian Ashokan art depicts the lion's roar with four lions looking in the four directions, which symbolizes the idea of having no back. Every direction is a front, symbolizing all-pervading awareness. The fearlessness covers all directions. Once you begin to radiate your fearlessness, it is all-pervading, radiated in all directions. In the traditional iconography certain Buddhas are represented as having a thousand faces or a million faces, looking in all directions in panoramic awareness. Since they look everywhere, there is nothing to defend.

The lion's roar is fearlessness in the sense that every situation in life is workable. Nothing is rejected as bad or grasped as good. But everything we experience in our life-situations, any type of emotion, is workable. We can see quite clearly that trying to apply the reference point of credentials is useless. We have to really work into the situation completely and thoroughly. If we are extremely interested in eating food, really hungry, there is no time to read the menu because we want to eat. We really want to relate with food. So forget about the menu. It is an immediate interest, a direct relationship.

The basic point of the lion's roar is that, if we are able to deal with emotions directly, able to relate with them as workable, then there is no need for external aid or explanations. It is a self-maintained situation. Any help from outsiders becomes credentials. So self-existing help develops. At that point, one does not need to avoid the credential problem any more, because there is no room for speculation or rationalization. Everything becomes obvious and immediate, workable. And there is no chance or time or space to speculate on how to become a charlatan, how to con other people, because the situation is so immediate. So the idea of charlatanism does not appear at all, because there is no room for the idea of a game.

Working with Negativity

WE ALL EXPERIENCE negativity—the basic aggression of wanting things to be different than they are. We cling, we defend, we attack, and throughout there is a sense of one's own wretchedness, and so we blame the world for our pain. This is negativity. We experience it as terribly unpleasant, foul-smelling, something we want to get rid of. But if we look into it more deeply, it has a very juicy smell and is very alive. Negativity is not bad *per se*, but something living and precise, connected with reality.

Negativity breeds tension, friction, gossip, discontentment, but it is also very accurate, deliberate and profound. Unfortunately, the heavy-handed interpretations and judgments we lay on these experiences obscure this fact. These interpretations and judgments are negative negativity, watching ourselves being negative and then deciding that the negativity is justified in being there. The negativity seems good-natured, with all sorts of good qualities in it, so we pat its back, guard it and justify it. Or if we are blamed or attacked by others, we interpret their negativity as being good for us. In either case the watcher, by commenting, interpreting and judging, is camouflaging and hardening the basic negativity.

Negative negativity refers to the philosophies and rationales we use to justify avoiding our own pain. We would like to pretend that these "evil" and "foul-smelling" aspects of ourselves and our world are not really there, or that they should not be there, or even that they *should* be there. So negative negativity is usually self-justifying, self-contained. It allows nothing to pierce its protective shell—a self-righteous way of trying to pretend that things are what we would like them to be instead of what they are.

This secondary, commenting kind of intelligence of double negativity is very cautious and cowardly as well as frivolous and emotional. It inhibits identification with the energy and intelligence of basic negativity. So let's forget about justifying ourselves, trying to prove to ourselves how good we are.

The basic honesty and simplicity of negativity can be creative in community as well as in personal relationships. Basic negativity is very revealing, sharp and accurate. If we leave it as basic negativity rather than overlaying it with conceptualizations, then we see the nature of its intelligence. Negativity breeds a great deal of energy, which clearly seen becomes intelligence. When we leave the energies as they are with their natural qualities, they are living rather than conceptualized. They strengthen our everyday lives.

The conceptualized negativity, the negative negativity, must be cut through. It deserves to be murdered on the spot with the sharp blow of basic intelligence— *prajnaparamita.* That is what *prajna* is for: to cut through intelligence when it changes into intellectual speculation or is based upon a belief of some kind. Beliefs are reinforced endlessly by other beliefs and dogmas, theological or moral or practical or business-like. That kind of intelligence should be killed on the spot, "uncompassionately." This is when compassion should not be idiot compassion. This intellectual energy should be shot, killed, squashed, razed to dust on the spot with one blow. That one blow of basic intelligence is direct compassion. The way to do this does not evolve out of intellectualizing or trying to find a way to justify yourself; but it just comes as the conclusion of basic intelligence and from a feeling of the texture of the situation.

For instance, if you walk on the snow or ice, you feel the texture of it the minute you put your foot down. You feel whether or not your shoe is going to grip. It is the feeling of texture, the richness of texture that we are talking about. If it is negative negativity, then there will be certain ways to squash or murder it. Somehow the energy to do this comes from the basic negativity itself, rather than from some special technique or ability for assassination. There is a time to be philosophical and a time to be soft. There is also a time to be "uncompassionate" and ruthless in dealing with these frivolous situations.

Frivolousness refers to the extra and unnecessary mental and physical acts with which we keep ourselves busy in order not to see what actually is happening in a situation. Whenever there is a frivolous emotional situation and concept growing out of it, then this ground should be completely extinguished with a direct blow—that is, by seeing directly what is not right and wholesome. This is what is called the Sword of Manjushri, which cuts the root of dualistic conceptualization with one blow. Here a person should really be "uncompassionate" and illogical. The real objective is just to squash the frivolousness, the unwillingness to see things as they actually are, which appears rational. Frivolousness does not really get a chance to feel the whole ground. It is preoccupied with reacting to your projections as they bounce back at you. True spontaneity feels the texture of the situation because it is less involved with self-consciousness, the attempt to secure oneself in a given situation.

It is obvious that, when you are really squashing frivolousness, you should feel pain, because there is a certain attraction toward the occupation of being frivolous. By squashing it you are completely taking away the occupation. You begin to feel that you have nothing to hold on to any more, which is rather frightening as well as painful. What do you do then, after you have extinguished everything? Then you must not live on your heroism, on having achieved something, but just dance with the continuing process of energy that has been liberated by this destruction.

The tantric tradition of Buddhism describes four actions or *karma-yogas*. The first is the action of "pacifying" a situation if it is not right. Pacifying is trying to feel the ground very softly. You feel the situation further and further, not just pacifying superficially, but expressing the whole, feeling it altogether. Then you expand your luscious, dignified and rich quality throughout. This is "enriching," the second karma. If that does not work, then "magnetizing" is the third karma. You bring the elements of the situation together. Having felt them out by pacifying and enriching them, you bring them together. If that is unsuccessful, then there is the action of "destroying" or extinguishing, the fourth karma.

These four karmas are very pertinent to the process of dealing with negativity and so-called problems. First pacify, then enrich, then magnetize, and if that does not work, finally extinguish, destroy altogether. This last is necessary only when the negative negativity uses a strong pseudo-logic or a pseudo-philosophical attitude or conceptualization. It is necessary when there is a notion of some kind which brings a whole succession of other notions, like the layers of an onion, or when one is using logic and ways of justifying oneself so that situations become very heavy and very solid. We know this heaviness is taking place, but simultaneously we play tricks on ourselves, feeling that we enjoy the heaviness of this logic, feeling that we need to have some occupation. When we begin to play this kind of game, there is no room. Out! It is said in the tantric tradition that, if you do not destroy when necessary, you are breaking the vow of compassion which actually commits you to destroying frivolousness. Therefore, keeping to the path does not necessarily mean only trying to be good and not offending anyone; it does not mean that, if someone obstructs our path, we should try to be polite to them and say "please" and "thank you." That does not work, that is not the point. If anyone gets abruptly in our path, we just push them out because their intrusion was frivolous. The path of dharma is not a good, sane, passive and "compassionate" path at all. It is a path on which no one should walk blindly. If they do—Out! They should be awakened by being excluded.

At the very advanced levels of practice we can go through the negative negativity and turn it into the original negativity so that we have a very powerful negative force that is pure and unself-conscious. That is, once having squashed this negative negativity altogether, having gone through the operation without anaesthesia, then we re-invite the negativity for the sake of energy. But this could be tricky.

If the pure energy of negativity is involved with any

form of ground, then it is always regarded as the property of the secondary, logical energy of negative negativity. This is because of our fascination to relive the basic negativity, to recreate the comfort and occupation of basic negativity. So there should not be any reliving of the occupation at all. Occupations should be completely cleared away. Then the energy which destroys the reliving of occupation turns out to be logical energy transmuted into crazy wisdom—conceptual ideas, let loose. That is to say, there are no more conceptual ideas, but only energy run wild. Originally there were conceptual ideas and then they were cut through altogether, so that you no longer regarded light and dark as light and dark; it becomes the non-dualistic state.

Then negativity simply becomes food, pure strength. You no longer relate to negativity as being good or bad, but you continually use the energy which comes out of it as a source of life so that you are never really defeated in a situation. Crazy wisdom cannot be defeated. If someone attacks or if someone praises, crazy wisdom will feed on either equally. As far as crazy wisdom is concerned, both praise and blame are the same thing because there is always some energy occurring . . . a really terrifying thought.

Crazy wisdom could become satanic but somehow it doesn't. Those who fear crazy wisdom destroy themselves. The negative destruction they throw at it bounces back at them, for crazy wisdom has no notion of good or bad or destruction or creation at all. Crazy wisdom cannot exist without communication, without a situation with which to work: whatever needs to be destroyed, it destroys; whatever needs to be cared for, it cares for. Hostility destroys itself and openness also opens itself. It depends on the situation. Some people may learn from destruction and some people may learn from creation. That is what the wrathful and peaceful deities, the *mahakalas* and the buddhas, symbolize.

The four arms of the mahakala (in the *thangka* which accompanies this chapter) represent the four karmas. The whole structure of the image is based on energy and complete compassion devoid of idiot compassion. In this particular thangka, the left arm represents pacifying. It holds a skull cup of *amrita,* the intoxicating nectar of the gods which is a means of pacification. Another arm holds a hooked knife which symbolizes enriching, extending your influence over others, feeling the texture of the ground and the richness. The hooked knife is also regarded as the sceptre of the gods. The third arm, on the right, holds a sword which is the tool for gathering energies together. The sword need not strike, but just through its being waved around energies come together. The fourth arm holds the three-pronged spear which symbolizes destruction. You do not have to destroy three times, but with one thrust of this spear you make three wounds, the ultimate destruction of ignorance, passion and aggression simultaneously.

The mahakala sits on the corpses of demons, which represents the paralysis of ego. This is very interesting and relates to what we have already discussed. You must not make an impulsive move into any situation. Let the situation come, then look at it, chew it properly, digest it, sit on it. The sudden move is unhealthy, impulsive and frivolous rather than spontaneous.

Spontaneity sees situations as they are. You see, there is a difference between spontaneity and frivolousness, a very thin line dividing them. Whenever there is an impulse to do something, you should not just do it; you should work with the impulse. If you are working with it, then you will not act frivolously; you want really to see it and taste it properly, devoid of frivolousness. Frivolousness means reacting according to reflex. You throw something and when it bounces back you react. Spontaneity is when you throw something and watch it and work with the energy when it bounces back at you. Frivolousness involves too much anxiety. Once you are emotionally worked up, then too much anxiety is put into your action. But when you are spontaneous, there is less anxiety and you just deal with situations as they are. You do not simply react, but you work with the quality and structure of the reaction. You feel the texture of the situation rather than just acting impulsively.

The mahakala is surrounded by flames representing the tremendous unceasing energy of anger without hatred, the energy of compassion. The skull crown symbolizes the negativities or emotions which are not destroyed or abandoned or condemned for being "bad." Rather they are used by the mahakala for his ornaments and crown.

V
Meditation
in Action

Work

WHEN YOU SEE ordinary situations with extraordinary insight it is like discovering a jewel in rubbish.
If work becomes part of your spiritual practice, then
your regular, daily problems cease to be only problems
and become a source of inspiration. Nothing is rejected
as ordinary and nothing is taken as being particularly
sacred, but all the substance and material available in
life-situations is used.

However, work can also be an escape from creativity.
Either you work frantically, filling in all the spaces and
not allowing any spontaneity to develop or else you are
lazy, regarding work as something to revolt against, which
indicates a fear of creativity. Instead of letting the creative process be, you follow your next preconception,
fearing a spacious state of mind. Whenever a person feels
depressed or is afraid or the situation is not going
smoothly, immediately he begins polishing a table or
weeding the garden, trying to distract himself. He does
not want to deal with the underlying problem so he seeks
a kind of pleasure of the moment. He is frightened of the
space, of any empty corner. Whenever there is an empty
wall, he puts up another picture or hanging. And the
more crowded his walls are, the more comfortable he feels.

83

True work is acting practically, relating to the earth directly. You could be working in the garden, in the house, washing dishes or doing whatever demands your attention. If you do not feel the relationship between earth and yourself, then the situation is going to turn chaotic. If you do not feel that every step, every situation reflects your state of mind, and therefore has spiritual significance, then the pattern of your life becomes full of problems, and you begin to wonder where these problems come from. They seem to spring from nowhere because you refuse to see the subtlety of life. Somehow, you cannot cheat, you cannot pretend to pour a cup of tea beautifully, you cannot act it. You must actually feel it, feel the earth and your relationship to it.

The Japanese tea ceremony is a good example of action that is in contact with earth. It begins by deliberately collecting the bowl, the napkin, the brush, the tea, and the boiling water. Tea is served and the guests drink deliberately, with a feeling of dealing with things properly. The ceremony also includes how to clean the bowls, how to put them away, how to finish properly. Clearing away is as important as starting.

It is extremely important to work, as long as you are not using work as an escape, as a way of ignoring the basic existence of a problem, particularly if you are interested in spiritual development. Work is one of the most subtle ways of acquiring discipline. You should not look down on someone who works in a factory or produces materialistic things. You learn a tremendous amount from such people. I think that many of our attitudinal problems about work come from a pseudo-sophistication of the analytic mind. You do not want to involve yourself physically at all. You want only to work intellectually or mentally.

This is a spiritual problem. Usually people interested in spiritual development think in terms of the importance of mind, that mysterious, high and deep thing that we have decided to learn about. But strangely enough the profound and the transcendental are to be found in the factory. It may not fill you with bliss to look at it, it may not sound as good as the spiritual experiences that we have read about, but somehow reality is to be found there, in the way in which we relate with everyday problems. If we relate to them in a simple, earthy way, we will work in a more balanced manner, and things will be dealt with properly. If we are able to simplify ourselves to that extent, then we will be able to see the neurotic aspect of mind much more clearly. The whole pattern of thought, the internal game that goes on, becomes much less of a game. It becomes a very practical way of thinking in situations.

Awareness in work is very important. It could be the same sort of awareness one has in sitting meditation, the leap of experiencing the openness of space. This depends very much upon feeling the earth and the space together. You cannot feel earth unless you feel space. The more you feel the space, the more you feel the earth. The feeling of space between you and objects becomes a natural product of awareness, of openness, of peace and lightness. And the way to practice is not to concentrate upon things nor to try to be aware of yourself and the job at the same time, but you should have a general feeling of acknowledging this openness as you are working. Then you begin to feel that there is more room in which to do things, more room in which to work. It is a question of acknowledging the existence of the openness of a continual meditative state. You don't have to try to hold on to it or try to bring it about deliberately, but just acknowledge that vast energy of openness with a fraction-of-a-second flash to it. After acknowledging, then almost deliberately ignore its existence and continue your work. The openness will continue and you will begin to develop the actual feeling of the things with which you are working. The awareness that we are speaking of is not so much a question of constant awareness as of an object of mind, but it is a matter of becoming one with awareness, becoming one with open space. This means becoming one with the actual things with which you are dealing as well. So meditation becomes very easy; it is no longer an attempt to split yourself into different sections and different degrees of awareness, the watcher and the doer. You begin to have a real relationship with external objects and their beauty.

Love

THERE IS A vast store of energy which is not centered, which is not ego's energy at all. It is this energy which is the centerless dance of phenomena, the universe interpenetrating and making love to itself. It has two characteristics: a fire quality of warmth and a tendency to flow in a particular pattern, in the same way in which fire contains a spark as well as the air which directs the spark. And this energy is always on-going, whether or not it is seen through the confused filter of ego. It cannot be destroyed or interrupted at all. It is like the ever-burning sun. It consumes everything to the point where it allows no room for doubt or manipulation.

But when this heat is filtered through ego, it becomes stagnant, because we ignore the basic ground, refuse to see the vast space in which this energy occurs. Then the energy cannot flow freely in the open space shared with the object of passion. Instead it is solidified, narrowed and directed by the central headquarters of ego to move outward in order to draw the object of passion into its territory. This captive energy extends out to its object and then returns to be programmed again. We extend our tentacles and try to fix our relationship. This attempt to cling to the situation makes the communication process superficial. We just touch another person's surface and get stuck there, never experiencing their whole being. We are blinded by our clinging. The object of passion, instead of being bathed in the intense warmth of free passion feels oppressed by the stifling heat of neurotic passion.

Free passion is radiation without a radiator, a fluid, pervasive warmth that flows effortlessly. It is not destructive because it is a balanced state of being and highly intelligent. Self-consciousness inhibits this intelligent, balanced state of being. By opening, by dropping our self-conscious grasping, we see not only the surface of an object, but we see the whole way through. We appreciate not in terms of sensational qualities alone, but we see in terms of whole qualities, which are pure gold. We are not overwhelmed by the exterior, but seeing the exterior simultaneously puts us through to the interior. So we reach the heart of the situation and, if this is a meeting of two people, the relationship is very inspiring because we do not see the other person purely in terms of physical attraction or habitual patterns, we see the inside as well as the outside.

This whole-way-through communication might produce a problem. Suppose you see right through someone and that person does not want you to see right through and becomes horrified with you and runs away. Then what to do? You have made your communication completely and thoroughly. If that person runs away from you, that is his way of communicating with you. You would not investigate further. If you did pursue and chase him, then sooner or later you would become a demon from that person's point of view. You see right through his body and he has juicy fat and meat that you would like to eat up, so you seem like a vampire to him. And the more you try to pursue the other person, the more you fail. Perhaps you looked through too sharply with your desire, perhaps you were too penetrating. Possessing beautiful keen eyes, penetrating passion and intelligence, you abused your talent, played with it. It is quite natural with people, if they possess some particular power or gifted energy, to abuse that quality, to misuse it by trying to penetrate every corner. Something quite obviously is lacking in such an approach—a sense of humor. If you try to push things too far, it means you do not feel the area properly; you only feel your relationship to the area. What is wrong is that you do not see all sides of the situation and therefore miss the humorous and ironical aspect.

Sometimes people run away from you because they want to play a game with you. They do not want a straight, honest and serious involvement with you, they want to play. But if they have a sense of humor and you do not, you become demonic. This is where *lalita*, the dance, comes in. You dance with reality, dance with apparent phenomena. When you want something very badly you do not extend your eye and hand automatically; you just admire. Instead of impulsively making a move from your side, you allow a move from the other side, which is learning to dance with the situation. You do not have to create the whole situation; you just watch it, work with it and learn to dance with it. So then it does not become your creation, but rather a mutual dance. No one is self-conscious, because it is a mutual experience.

When there is a fundamental openness in a relationship, being faithful, in the sense of real trust, happens automatically; it is a natural situation. Because the communication is so real and so beautiful and flowing, you cannot communicate in the same way with someone else, so automatically you are drawn together. But if any doubt presents itself, if you begin to feel threatened by some abstract possibility, although your communication is going beautifully at the time, then you are sowing the seed of paranoia and regarding the communication purely as ego entertainment.

If you sow a seed of doubt, it may make you rigid and terrified, afraid of losing the communication which is so good and real. And at some stage you will begin to be bewildered as to whether the communication is loving or aggressive. This bewilderment brings a certain loss of distance, and in this way neurosis begins. Once you lose the right perspective, the right distance in the communication process, then love becomes hate. The natural thing with hatred, just as with love, is that you want to make physical communication with the person; that is, you want to kill or injure them. In any relationship in which the ego is involved, a love relationship or any other, there is always the danger of turning against your partner. As long as there is the notion of threat or insecurity of any kind, then a love relationship could turn into its opposite.

Working with People

THE IDEA OF helping each other is more subtle than we might think. Generally, when we try to help other people, we make a nuisance of ourselves, make demands upon them. The reason we make a nuisance of ourselves to other people is that we cannot stand ourselves. We want to burst out into something, to make it known that we are desperate. So we extend ourselves and step out into someone else's territory without permission. We want to make a big deal of ourselves, no matter if the other person wants to accept us or not. We do not really want to expose our basic character, but we want to dominate the situation around us. We march straight through into another person's territory, disregarding the proper conditions for entering it. There might be signs saying, "Keep off the grass, no trespassing." But each time we see these signs, they make us more aggressive, more revolutionary. We just push ourselves into the other person's territory, like a tank going through a wall. We are not only committing vandalism to someone else's territory, but we are disrupting our own territory as well —it is inward vandalism too. It is being a nuisance to ourselves as well as to others.

Most people hate being in this situation. They do not want to feel that they are making a nuisance of themselves. On the other hand, one does not have to adopt a cool facade and a genteel manner and do everything correctly and be polite and considerate. True consideration is not diplomacy, putting on a facade of smiles or polite conversation. It is something more than that. It requires much energy and intelligence. It requires opening up our territory rather than marching into someone else's. It requires not playing magnetizing or repelling games, not surrounding our territory with electric wire or magnets. Then there is a faint possibility that we could be of some use to someone else. But we still should be tentative about helping others. We have glimpsed the first step in genuinely helping others, but it takes a lot of time to pick up the thing, put it in our mouth, chew it, taste it and swallow it. It takes a long time to take our fences down. The first step is to learn to love ourselves, make friends with ourselves, not torture ourselves any more. And the second step is to communicate to people, to establish a relationship and gradually help them. It takes a long time and a long process of disciplined patience.

If we learn to not make a nuisance of ourselves and then to open ourselves to other people, then we are ready for the third stage—selfless help. Usually when we help someone, we are looking for something in return. We might say to our children, "I want you to be happy, therefore I'm putting all my energy into you," which implies that, "I want you to be happy because I want you to provide me with entertainment; bring me happiness, because I want to be happy." In the third stage of selfless help, true compassion, we do not do things because it gives us pleasure but because things need to be done.

Our response is selfless, noncentralized. It is not for them or for me. It is environmental generosity.

But we cannot just go out and try to practice this kind of compassion. First we must learn how not to make a nuisance of ourselves. If we can make friends with ourselves, if we are willing to be what we are, without hating parts of ourselves and trying to hide them, then we can begin to open to others. And if we can begin to open without always having to protect ourselves, then perhaps we can begin to really help others.

The Eightfold Path

THERE SEEM TO be so many sidetracks in relating to our life-situations, sidetracks of all kinds by which we are seduced: "Food, gas and lodging, next exit." We are always promised something if we turn right at the next exit as we travel down our highway. There are so many colorful advertisements. We never want to be just where and what we are; we always want to be somewhere else. We can always turn right at the next exit, even though we really know we are stuck on our highway anyway, that we really have no choice about it. Where we are is embarrassing, and so we would like to hear somebody say that there is an alternative whereby we do not have to be ashamed of ourselves: "I'll provide a mask, just put it on." Then you can get off at that exit and you are "saved" by pretending to be what you are not. You think people see you as a different person, the one wearing the mask of what you would like to be.

Buddhism promises nothing. It teaches us to be what we are where we are, constantly, and it teaches us to relate to our living situations accordingly. That seems to be the way to proceed on our highway without being distracted by the sidetracks and exits of all kinds. The signs say: "Tibetan Village, next exit;" "Japanese Village, next exit;" "Nirvana, next exit;" "Enlightenment, next exit—instant one;" "Disneyland, next exit." If you turn right, everything is going to be OK. You get what you are promised. But after having gone to Disneyland or having taken part in the Nirvana Festival, then you have to think about how you are going to get back to your car, how you are going to get home. This means you have to get back on the highway once more. It is unavoidable. I am afraid that this portrays our basic situation, the process in which we are constantly involved.

I am sorry not to be presenting any glamorous and beautiful promises. Wisdom happens to be a domestic affair. Buddha saw the world as it is and that was his enlightenment. "Buddha" means "awake," being awake, completely awake—that seems to be his message to us. He offered us a path to being awake, a path with eight points, and he called it "the eightfold path."

The first point the Buddha made has to do with "right view." Wrong view is a matter of conceptualization. Someone is walking toward us—suddenly we freeze. Not only do we freeze ourselves, but we also freeze the space in which the person is walking toward us. We call him "friend" who is walking through this space or "enemy." Thus the person is automatically walking through a frozen situation of fixed ideas—"this is that," or "this is

not that." This is what Buddha called "wrong view." It
is a conceptualized view which is imperfect because we
do not see the situation as it is. There is the possibility,
on the other hand, of not freezing that space. The person
could walk into a lubricated situation of myself and that
person as we are. Such a lubricated situation can exist
and can create open space.

Of course, openness could be appropriated as a philosophical concept as well, but the philosophy need not
necessarily be fixed. The situation could be seen without
the idea of lubrication as such, without any fixed idea.
In other words, the philosophical attitude could be just
to see the situation as it is. "That person walking toward
me is not a friend, therefore he is not an enemy either.
He is just a person approaching me. I don't have to pre-
judge him at all." That is what is called "right view."

The next aspect of the eightfold path is called "right
intention." Ordinary intention is based upon the process
we have just described. Having conceptually fixed the
person, now you are ready either to grasp or attack him.
Automatically there is an apparatus functioning to provide either a waterbed or a shotgun for that person. That
is the intention. It is a thought process which relates
thinking to acting. When you encounter a situation, you
think; and thinking inclines toward acting. In your constant alertness to relate the situation to your security, the
intention is worked between two jaws. The emotional
element, concerned with pleasure or pain, expansion or
withdrawal, is one jaw; the heavy, physical aspect of the
situation is the other. Situations keep you chewing your
intention constantly, like gristle. Intention always has
the quality of either invitation or attack.

But according to Buddha there is also "right inten-

tion." In order to see what this is, we first must understand what Buddha meant by "right." He did not mean
to say right as opposed to wrong at all. He said "right"
meaning "what is," being right without a concept of
what is right. "Right" translates the Sanskrit *samyak,*
which means "complete." Completeness needs no relative help, no support through comparison; it is self-
sufficient. Samyak means seeing life as it is without
crutches, straightforwardly. In a bar one says, "I would
like a straight drink." Not diluted with club soda or
water; you just have it straight. That is samyak. No
dilutions, no concoctions—just a straight drink. Buddha
realized that life could be potent and delicious, positive
and creative, and he realized that you do not need any
concoctions with which to mix it. Life is a straight drink
—hot pleasure, hot pain, straightforward, one hundred
percent.

So right intention means not being inclined toward
anything other than what is. You are not involved in the
idea that life *could be* beautiful or *could be* painful, and
you are not being careful about life. According to Buddha, life *is* pain, life *is* pleasure. That is the samyak
quality of it—so precise and direct: straight life without
any concoctions. There is no need at all to reduce life
situations or intensify them. Pleasure as it is, pain as it
is—these are the absolute qualities of Buddha's approach
to intention.

The third aspect of the eightfold path is "right
speech." In Sanskrit the word for speech is *vac,* which
means "utterance," "word," or "logos." It implies perfect communication, communication which says, "It is
so," rather than, "I think it is so." "Fire is hot," rather
than, "I think fire is hot." Fire *is* hot, automatically—

the direct approach. Such communication is true speech, in Sanskrit *satya,* which means "being true." It is dark outside at this time. Nobody would disagree with that. Nobody would have to say, "I think it is dark outside," or, "You must believe it is dark outside." You would just say, "It is dark outside." It is just the simple minimum of words we could use. It is true.

The fourth aspect of the eightfold path is "right morality" or "right discipline." If there is no one to impose discipline and no one to impose discipline on, then there is no need for discipline in the ordinary sense at all. This leads to the understanding of right discipline, complete discipline, which does not exist relative to ego. Ordinary discipline exists only at the level of relative decisions. If there is a tree, there must be branches; however, if there is no tree, there are no such things as branches. Likewise, if there is no ego, a whole range of projections becomes unnecessary. Right discipline is that kind of giving-up process; it brings us into complete simplicity.

We are all familiar with the samsaric kind of discipline which is aimed at self-improvement. We give up all kinds of things in order to make ourselves "better," which provides us with tremendous reassurance that we can *do* something with our lives. Such forms of discipline are just unnecessarily complicating your life rather than trying to simplify and live the life of a *rishi.*

"Rishi" is a Sanskrit word which refers to the person who constantly leads a straightforward life. The Tibetan word for "rishi" is *trangsong (drang sron)* . *Trang* means "direct," *song* means "upright." The term refers to one who leads a direct and upright life by not introducing new complications into his life-situation. This is a permanent discipline, the ultimate discipline. We simplify life rather than get involved with new gadgets or finding new concoctions with which to mix it.

The fifth point is "right livelihood." According to Buddha, right livelihood simply means making money by working, earning dollars, pounds, francs, pesos. To buy food and pay rent you need money. This is not a cruel imposition on us. It is a natural situation. We need not be embarrassed by dealing with money nor resent having to work. The more energy you put out, the more you get in. Earning money involves you in so many related situations that it permeates your whole life. Avoiding work usually is related to avoiding other aspects of life as well.

People who reject the materialism of American society and set themselves apart from it are unwilling to face themselves. They would like to comfort themselves with the notion that they are leading philosophically virtuous lives, rather than realizing that they are unwilling to work with the world as it is. We cannot expect to be helped by divine beings. If we adopt doctrines which lead us to expect blessings, then we will not be open to the real possibilities in situations. Buddha believed in cause and effect. For example, you get angry at your friend and decide to cut off the relationship. You have a hot argument with him and walk out of the room and slam the door. You catch your finger in the door. Painful, isn't it? That is cause and effect. You realize there is some warning there. You have overlooked karmic necessity. It happens all the time. This is what we run into when we violate right livelihood.

The sixth point is "right effort." The Sanskrit, *samyagvyayama*, means energy, endurance, exertion.

This is the same as the bodhisattva's principle of energy. There is no need to be continually just pushing along, drudging along. If you are awake and open in living situations, it is possible for them and you to be creative, beautiful, humorous and delightful. This natural openness is right effort, as opposed to any old effort. Right effort is seeing a situation precisely as it is at that very moment, being present fully, with delight, with a grin. There are occasions when we know we are present, but we do not really want to commit ourselves, but right effort involves full participation.

For right effort to take place we need gaps in our discursive or visionary gossip, room to stop and be present. Usually, someone is whispering some kind of seduction, some gossip behind our back; "It's all very well to meditate, but how about going to the movies? Meditating is nice, but how about getting together with our friends? How about that? Shall we read that book? Maybe we should go to sleep. Shall we go buy that thing we want? Shall we? Shall we? Shall we?" Discursive thoughts constantly happening, numerous suggestions constantly being supplied—effort has no room to take place. Or maybe it is not discursive thoughts at all. Sometimes it is a continual vision of possibilities: "My enemy is coming and I'm hitting him—I want war." Or, "My friend is coming, I'm hugging him, welcoming him to my house, giving him hospitality." It goes on all the time. "I have a desire to eat lambchops—no, leg of lamb, steak, lemon ice cream. My friend and I could go out to the shop and get some ice cream and bring it home and have a nice conversation over ice cream. We could go to that Mexican restaurant and get tacos 'to go' and bring them back home. We'll dip them in the sauce and eat together

and have a nice philosophical discussion as we eat. Nice
to do that with candlelight and soft music." We are constantly dreaming of infinite possibilities for all kinds of
entertainment. There is no room to stop, no room to
start providing space. Providing space: effort, non-effort
and effort, non-effort—it's very choppy in a sense, very
precise, knowing how to release the discursive or visionary gossip. Right effort—it's beautiful.

The next one is "right mindfulness." Right mindfulness does not simply mean being aware; it is like creating
a work of art. There is more spaciousness in right mindfulness than in right effort. If you are drinking a cup of
tea, you are aware of the whole environment as well as
the cup of tea. You can therefore trust what you are
doing, you are not threatened by anything. You have
room to dance in the space, and this makes it a creative
situation. The space is open to you.

The eighth aspect of the eightfold path is "right
samadhi," right absorption. Samadhi has the sense of
being as it is, which means relating with the space of a
situation. This pertains to one's living situation as well
as to sitting meditation. Right absorption is being completely involved, thoroughly and fully, in a non-dualistic
way. In sitting meditation the technique and you are
one; in life situations the phenomenal world is also part
of you. Therefore you do not have to meditate as such,
as though you were a person distinct from the act of
meditating and the object of meditation. If you are one
with the living situation as it is, your meditation just
automatically happens.

VI
The Open Way

The Bodhisattva Vow

BEFORE WE COMMIT ourselves to walking the bodhisattva path, we must first walk the hinayana or narrow path. This path begins formally with the student taking refuge in the buddha, the dharma and the sangha —that is, in the lineage of teachers, the teachings and the community of fellow pilgrims. We expose our neurosis to our teacher, accept the teachings as the path and humbly share our confusion with our fellow sentient beings. Symbolically, we leave our homeland, our property and our friends. We give up the familiar ground that supports our ego, admit the helplessness of ego to control its world and secure itself. We give up our clingings to superiority and self-preservation. But taking refuge does not mean becoming dependent upon our teacher or the community or the scriptures. It means giving up searching for a home, becoming a refugee, a lonely person who must depend upon himself. A teacher or fellow traveler or the scriptures might show us where we are on a map and where we might go from there, but we have to make the journey ourselves. Fundamentally, no one can help us. If we seek to relieve our loneliness, we will be distracted from the path. Instead, we must make a relation-

103

ship with loneliness until it becomes aloneness.

In the hinayana the emphasis is on acknowledging our confusion. In the mahayana we acknowledge that we are a buddha, an awakened one, and act accordingly, even though all kinds of doubts and problems might arise. In the scriptures, taking the bodhisattva vow and walking on the bodhisattva path is described as being the act of awakening bodhi or "basic intelligence." Becoming "awake" involves seeing our confusion more clearly. We can hardly face the embarrassment of seeing our hidden hopes and fears, our frivolousness and neurosis. It is such an overcrowded world. And yet it is a very rich display. The basic idea is that, if we are going to relate with the sun, we must also relate with the clouds that obscure the sun. So the bodhisattva relates positively to both the naked sun and the clouds hiding it. But at first the clouds, the confusion, which hide the sun are more prominent. When we try to disentangle ourselves, the first thing we experience is entanglement.

The stepping stone, the starting point in becoming awake, in joining the family of buddhas, is the taking of the bodhisattva vow. Traditionally, this vow is taken in the presence of a spiritual teacher and images of the buddhas and the scriptures in order to symbolize the presence of the lineage, the family of Buddha. One vows that from today until the attainment of enlightenment I devote my life to work with sentient beings and renounce my own attainment of enlightenment. Actually we cannot attain enlightenment until we give up the notion of "me" personally attaining it. As long as the enlightenment drama has a central character, "me," who has

certain attributes, there is no hope of attaining enlightenment because it is nobody's project; it is an extraordinarily strenuous project but nobody is pushing it. Nobody is supervising it or appreciating its unfolding. We
cannot pour our being from our dirty old vessel into a
new clean one. If we examine our old vessel, we discover
that it is not a solid thing at all. And such a realization
of egolessness can only come through the practice of
meditation, relating with discursive thoughts and gradually working back through the five skandhas. When
meditation becomes an habitual way of relating with
daily life, a person can take the bodhisattva vow. At that
point discipline has become ingrown rather than en-
forced. It is like becoming involved in an interesting
project upon which we automatically spend a great deal
of time and effort. No one needs to encourage or threaten
us; we just find ourselves intuitively doing it. Identifying
with buddha-nature is working with our intuition, with
our ingrown discipline.

The bodhisattva vow acknowledges confusion and
chaos—aggression, passion, frustration, frivolousness—as
part of the path. The path is like a busy, broad highway,
complete with roadblocks, accidents, construction work
and police. It is quite terrifying. Nevertheless it is ma-
jestic, it is the great path. "From today onward until the
attainment of enlightenment I am willing to live with
my chaos and confusion as well as with that of all other
sentient beings. I am willing to share our mutual confusion." So no one is playing a one-upmanship game.
The bodhisattva is a very humble pilgrim who works
in the soil of samsara to dig out the jewel embedded in it.

Heroism

THE BODHISATTVA PATH is an heroic path. In the countries in which it developed—Tibet, China, Japan, Mongolia—the people are rugged, hard-working and earthy. The style of practice of the mahayana reflects the heroic qualities of these people—the Japanese *samurai* tradition, the industriousness of the Chinese peasant, the Tibetan struggle with barren, forbidding land. However, in America the ruggedly heroic approach to practice of these peoples is often translated and distorted into a rigid militantism, a robot-like regimentation. The original approach involved the delight of feeling oneself invincible, of having nothing to lose, of being completely convinced of your aloneness. Sometimes, of course, beginning bodhisattvas have second thoughts about such a daring decision to abandon enlightenment and throw themselves to the mercy of sentient beings and work with them, taking delight and pride in compassionate action. They become frightened. This hesitation is described metaphorically in the *sutras* as standing in the doorway of your house, having one foot out in the street and the other foot inside the house. That moment is the test of whether you go beyond the hesitation and step out into the no-man's-land of the street or decide to step back into your familiar homeground, of whether you are willing to work for the benefit of all sentient beings or wish to indulge yourself in the *arhat* mentality of self-enlightenment.

The preparation for the bodhisattva path is the unification of body and mind: the body works for the mind and the mind works for the body. The hinayana shamatha and vipashyana practices make the mind precise, tranquil and smooth in the positive sense—precisely being there, rather than dreaming or sleeping or hazily perceiving. We can make a cup of tea properly, cook sunny-side-up properly, serve food properly, because the body and mind are synchronized.

Then we are ready to leap on to the bodhisattva path, to open to the joy of working with sentient beings, including oneself. The bodhisattva makes friends with himself as well as with others. There are no mysterious, dark corners left of which to be suspicious; no surprises can occur to destroy the bodhisattva's spiritual intelligence, his dignity and heroism. This is the first step, the first *bhumi** or spiritual level.

The word "bhumi" in Sanskrit, or the word *sa* in Tibetan, means "earth" or "level" or "ground," the ground where you can relate with yourself and others. There is no mystification, no confusion; it is obviously solid earth. In other words, it is the equivalent of the basic sanity, fundamentally being *there*. Since the bodhisattva knows his body and his mind and how to relate with the two, the whole process becomes "skillful means" because of such transcendental security. Which is more like being *in* security rather than being secured,

---

*A chart of the ten bhumis and their corresponding *paramitas* in Tibetan, Sanskrit and English is given in the Appendix.

rather than watching yourself to make sure everything is okay. That fundamental security comes from realizing that you have broken through something. You reflect back and realize that you used to be extraordinarily paranoid and neurotic, watching each step you made, thinking you might lose your sanity, that situations were always threatening in some way. Now you are free of all those fears and preconceptions. You discover that you have something to give rather than having to demand from others, having to grasp all the time. For the first time, you are a rich person, you contain basic sanity. You have something to offer, you are able to work with your fellow sentient beings, you do not have to reassure yourself anymore. Reassurance implies a mentality of poverty—you are checking yourself, "Do I have it? How could I do it?" But the bodhisattva's delight in his richness is based upon experience rather than theory or wishful thinking. It is *so,* directly, fundamentally. He is fundamentally rich and so can delight in generosity.

Thus the bodhisattva at the level of the first bhumi develops generosity. He is not acting generously in order to get something in return, but he is just being generous and warm. If you are acting kindly to someone in the conventional sense, it has the connotation of looking down upon someone lower, less fortunate than you. "I am rich and you need help because you are not like me." The bodhisattva's generosity need not be gentle and soothing; it could be very violent or sharp because he gives you what you need rather than what will please you superficially. He does not expect anything in return at all. He can be generous physically, giving food, wealth, clothes and shelter, or spiritually, giving food for the mind, restoring your mental health. The best kind of generosity according to the scriptures is that of working with another person's state of mind. But the bodhisattva does not go beyond his own understanding; he regards himself as a student rather than as a teacher. Nor does he try to seduce the object of his generosity. He is aware not only of "me and them" but also of the space that both the giver and the receiver are sharing. The perception of the shared space is the operation of the sharp intelligence of prajna.

The joyous generosity of the first bhumi is accompanied by prajna, transcendental knowledge. This knowledge is the result of vipashyana practice, the basic training you inherited from your hinayana practice. Opening to the joyous richness of the first bhumi automatically brings transcendental knowledge as well. Prajna is often translated as "wisdom," but it is preferable to translate it as "transcendental knowledge" and to use the word wisdom to refer to *jnana,* the meditative state at the level of tantra which is more advanced than prajna.

At the level of the first bhumi, prajna involves cutting through, dissolving the boundary between meditation and non-meditation. The sense of someone being there, someone being "aware" does not occur. The bodhisattva might still practice his discipline of sitting meditation, but he begins to find it irrelevant in some sense; it is just a disciplinary act. In actual fact his arising from meditation and participating in daily life does not change his mental state at all. His acts of generosity go on all the time. In other words, the bodhisattva already has the sharpness, the intelligence of the awakened state of mind. That is why his generosity becomes *dana paramita. Dana* means "generosity," *para* means "other," *mita* means "shore." It is generosity that transcends, that goes to the other shore. You go beyond the river of samsara, the river of confusion, the continual chain reaction pattern of karma in which each flow initiates the next flow like an electric current in which each spark of electricity is independent but initiates the next.

Prajna is transcendence, cutting through the volitional chain reaction of karma. But the act of cutting through the karmic chain might itself generate some chain reaction, because you are cutting something and acknowledging the cutting through. It becomes very subtle. Until the bodhisattva reaches the tenth bhumi he cannot completely cut the chain of karmic bondage because he is acknowledging the very act of cutting through. Prajna is knowledge in the sense that you still regard the dharma or the knowledge as external to yourself; there is still confirmation of the experience, one still experiences cutting through as an event that gives you information, an event from which you learn. The bodhisattva must go through ten stages of development to cut through the watcher, the acknowledger. The rejoicing process of the first bhumi is celebrating getting away from samsara rather than getting beyond it, so the bodhisattva still carries elements of samsara with him constantly.

The first bhumi is described in the scriptures as a state in which you have drunk half a cup of tea and still have half left. You have selected the tea, brewed it, tasted it and begun to drink it, but you still have not drunk the whole cup of tea. You are stuck, though not in the sense of being trapped, but you still have to work through the drinking of the other half of the cup, which takes ten steps to complete. Then you must clean your cup and put it back where it belongs.

The Sanity of Earth

THE SECOND BHUMI is called the "spotless" bhumi, and it involves the *shila paramita* of "morality" or "discipline." The purity of the bodhisattva referred to by the shila paramita is based upon making friends with oneself, loving oneself. You are not a nuisance to yourself anymore; you are good company, an inspiration to yourself. You do not have to control yourself so as to avoid temptations or follow rules or laws. You find temptations less relevant and guidelines less necessary, because you naturally follow the appropriate patterns. There is no need to try to be pure, to painfully discipline yourself to be pure, to apply detergent to your natural condition. The spotlessness or purity of the second bhumi is realized when you acknowledge your natural purity.

It is like feeling naturally at home in a clean, orderly place. You do not have to fit yourself into it; if you try to fit yourself in, you become rigid and create chaos. So the morality of the bodhisattva is a natural process. Unskillful action becomes irrelevant. The bodhisattva delights in working with people rather than regarding compassionate action as a duty. He has no dogma about how he should act or how other people should be. He does not try to reform or transform anyone because they do not fit his model. If people are determined to con-

vert others into their mold, then they are attempting to
reassure themselves by using the convert to relieve their
doubt. The bodhisattva is not concerned with conver-
sion; he respects others' lifestyles, speaks their language
and allows them to evolve according to their nature
rather than making them into a replica of himself. It
requires tremendous discipline to avoid converting people. The bodhisattva will experience strong impulses to
tell people how things ought to be. But instead of acting
on these impulses, the bodhisattva regards them as manure to work through, an expression of his insecurity.
He no longer needs that kind of reinforcement.

One type of discipline known as the "gathering of virtue" is connected with relating to physical things. Because the bodhisattva has been well trained in shamatha
and vipashyana meditation, he does not relate to a cup
of tea by knocking it over. He picks it up, drinks it, and
puts it down properly. There is no frivolousness involved. The *Bodhicaryavatara* notes that, when the
bodhisattva decides to relax and sit on the ground, he
does not make doodles with the dust on the ground. He
does not need to entertain himself restlessly. He is just
sitting there. Making doodles would seem an effort to
him. I hope you do not take it too seriously, that if you
make doodles you are not a potential bodhisattva. The
idea is that, if you are respectful of your environment,
you will take care of it, not treat it frivolously. As a
cameraman respects his cameras or a professor his books,
so the bodhisattva respects the earth. Frivolousness is
arduous to him. There is an "old dog" quality, a "sitting
bull" quality; he is just being there, precisely, properly.
Making an additional move is frivolous. Of course he
may be very active as well as peaceful, but he would not

give in to a sudden outburst of energy; his action is deliberate and sane, deliberate in the sense of not being impulsive.

The bodhisattva's discipline is to relate to earth properly, to relate to his senses and mind properly. He is not concerned with psychic phenomena or other worlds. Ignoring earth to chase after psychic phenomena is like the play of children trying to find gold at the end of a rainbow. We do not have to concern ourselves with the cosmic world, the world of gods, psychic powers, angels and devils. To do so may be to lose track of the physical world in which we live, and this results in madness. The test of the bodhisattva's sanity is how directly he relates to earth. Anything else is a sidetrack.

Patience

BEFORE WE DISCUSS the third bhumi, I would like to point out that the ten stages of the bodhisattva's path toward enlightenment should be regarded as landmarks, points of reference on a map, rather than as events to be celebrated, such as birthdays or graduations. There are no medals for achievement along the bodhisattva path. Each stage, even enlightenment itself, is like the different stages in the growth of a tree. The first bhumi is an extremely spectacular experience, a sudden explosion of joy, realizing that you could be generous, you could open, but beyond that the other bhumis are less spectacular. One bhumi develops to a peak point, and then gradually the next bhumi suggests itself and you cross the border very gently and arrive at the beginning of the next bhumi. It is frivolous to ask what bhumi you are in or to develop courses aimed at achieving the various levels. It is a very gentle, very gradual process.

Patience, the paramita connected with the third bhumi, is particularly related with the idea that the bodhisattva does not desire to be a buddha but would rather work with sentient beings to save them from their confusion. Patience also implies heroism in the sense of having nothing to lose. The meditation practice connected with patience is working with territory. There is no territory that is yours or that is others'; everyone is in no-man's-land. Not seeking enlightenment for ego's personal benefit, you have no need for territory so your space becomes a public park, a common ground, no-man's-land. No-man's-land is free ground, not subject to the laws of any government. You are free to do anything there, no one can make any demands upon you, so you can afford to wait, to be patient. Because there are no obligations you are free from time, not in the sense of being oblivious to what time it might be, but in the sense of not being compulsively driven by obligations to keep within time limits.

Patience does not mean forbearance in the sense of enduring pain, allowing someone to torture you at his leisure. The bodhisattva would strike down his torturer and defend himself, which is common-sense sanity. In fact the bodhisattva's blow would be more powerful because it would not be impulsive or frivolous. The bodhisattva has great power because nothing can shake him;

his action is calm, deliberate and persevering. Since there is space between himself and others, he does not feel threatened, but he is very careful. He scans the whole environment for things which need to be dealt with. Both patience and intelligent caution are operating in no-man's-land. So the bodhisattva can spring out like a tiger and claw you, bite you, crush you. He is not inhibited by conventional morality or idiot compassion. He is not afraid to subjugate what needs to be subjugated, to destroy what needs to be destroyed, and to welcome that which needs to be welcomed.

The conventional notion of patience is to be very kind and wait and hold your temper, repressing your restlessness. If we are waiting for someone, we smoke cigarettes, read, pace back and forth to keep ourselves cool. When they say, "I'm sorry I'm late," we say, "Don't mention it. I've been enjoying myself, looking at the scenery, talking to strangers. Let's get to our business, I'm glad you're here." Although we pretend that we are not concerned about the time, actually we are compulsively caught up in living by the clock so our denial of concern and the hiding of our anger is hypocritical. The bodhisattva, on the other hand, free from the compulsive concern with time, can just sit patiently without feeling that he is "waiting" for something else to happen. Although there is a sense of timelessness in the bodhisattva's action, this does not mean that he does everything so slowly that his action is inefficient. In fact, he is very efficient because his action is direct and persevering. Nothing sidetracks him, nothing scares him. He does not complain in the conventional sense, but he does point out discrepancies in organization or in the neurosis of workers. He does not complain about them, but he just relates to them as facts, as things that need correction. This sounds like a good strategy for a businessman to adopt, but unless a person has surrendered to the whole process of treading the path, it is not possible to be patient in this way.

Tradition

Virya, the paramita of the fourth bhumi, is taking delight in and working hard with whatever working base or material we are presented with—our state of mind, our traditions, our society. It is not taking sides for or against our traditions or our state of mind, but it is taking delight in them and then working with them. It is not enough to reject superficially the different aspects of the world around us. It is too simple-minded just to abandon traditional morality as being old-fashioned, like an old clothing style, and then substitute a swinging morality, an up-to-date, "mod" morality. Many of the young reject tradition altogether, even the smell of it. They see no truth in it at all. "I'm unhappy, neurotic because of them—my parents, my teachers, the media, the politicians, the psychiatrists, the capitalists, the clergymen, the computers, the scientists." We denounce the government, the schools, the churches, the synagogues, the hospitals. But there is some uncertainty in this stance. Perhaps there could be some truth in what the establishment says, in the way it does things? "Well, if there is, I'll pick only what is meaningful to me and reject the rest. I'll interpret tradition my way." We want to justify our existence as a good person, a little Christ or Buddha. This self-conscious attempt to define our identity or style is another form of spiritual materialism. We get a kick out of a certain style and self-justification from certain ideas that clothe our rebellion in glamorous imagery.

The bodhisattva, on the other hand, firmly roots himself in the traditions of his society but does not feel obligated to follow them. He is not afraid to take a new step, but the reason he is stepping out of the tradition is because he knows it so well. His inspiration to step out comes from that tradition. First we must step into the tradition, must understand it fully, its wise and its foolish aspects, why people are hypnotized by its dogmas; we must understand what wisdom, if any, lies behind the dogma. Then we can step out of it sanely.

The traditional approach to being a good person is to eliminate all color, all spectacle. You camouflage yourself and blend into the social landscape; you become white. White is associated with purity, cleanliness, gentleness, presentableness. But to be an extraordinarily good citizen you need to add color to the basic white. To improve society you need some color to contrast with the white.

So the bodhisattva is not bound by white, by law, by convention or by traditional morality, but neither does he kill someone on the spot because he feels some faint aggression toward him, nor does he make love to a woman on the street because he feels passion toward her. The conventional approach is to hesitate out of fear of embarrassment or a sense of impropriety or vice. "I shouldn't do it, it's wrong." There is a faint suggestion and the rejection of the suggestion, which is depressing.

"I wish I could, but society or my conscience does not permit me." But perhaps there is something more to our hesitation, perhaps it is our basic sanity that keeps us from acting impulsively.

Sanity lies somewhere between the inhibitions of conventional morality and the looseness of extreme impulse, but the area in-between is very fuzzy. The bodhisattva delights in the play between hesitation and extreme impulsiveness—it is beautiful to look at—so delight in itself is the approach of sanity. Delight is to open our eyes to the totality of the situation rather than siding with this or that point of view. The bodhisattva does not side with rejecting convention, mocking everything out of sheer frustration, trying to get the world to acknowledge him. Nor does he side with blind dogma, holding back out of fear, trying to mold the world to conform to rigid ideas and rules. The bodhisattva takes delight in polarities but does not side with any extreme. He accepts what is there as the message and explores it further and further, and the conflict between polarities becomes his inspiration. In order to be a communist you must have a model of what not to be, which means you must understand capitalism, so capitalism is your inspiration.

The bodhisattva's inspiration is the war between the awakened mentality and the samsaric mentality: the samsaric mentality is the inspiration for the awakened mentality. We need not change ourselves, need not negate what we are. We can use what we are as inspiration. So virya, the fourth bhumi, is taking delight in and working hard with whatever working base we have— our neurosis, our sanity, our culture, our society. We do not make sectarian distinctions or assert our superiority, but we take delight in what is and then work with it.

Zen and Prajna

THE PARAMITA OF the fifth bhumi is panoramic awareness. This meditative state has been called *dhyana* in the Indian tradition, *ch'an* in the Chinese tradition, and *zen* in the Japanese tradition. They all mean a state of total involvement, without center or fringe. If there is a center and a fringe, then our state of mind ceases to be one of total involvement because we have to keep track of both ends; a sense of polarity is always present.

So dhyana or zen is awareness without a watcher. In the superficial sense, when we speak of awareness, we mean egocentric watching, knowing what we are doing, knowing where we are supposed to be and how we handle the situation, which is quite a complicated process. We have to keep track of ourselves and our situation, keep track of how we are handling it and how the situation is affected by our action. There are so many things to manage at one time that we fear losing control, so we have to be extraordinarily alert and careful. Trying to be totally aware in this way is very difficult and complicated.

Awareness in the sense of zen is much simpler. The Tibetan word for it is *samten* (*bsam gtan*) : *sam* means "awareness," *ten* means "making stable." So samten means "stable awareness," sane awareness rather than neurotic awareness, awareness in the sense that there are very few things to keep track of because everything has been simplified into one situation. If there is simplicity

and spaciousness, then the bodhisattva actions, the paramitas, generosity, patience, energy, discipline, and so
on, are seen to be distinct processes. And if these processes take place in a very open situation, then there is
no conflict between generosity and patience and the rest;
they can be combined together to complement each
other.

The spaciousness of dhyana or "panoramic awareness" inspires the further development of prajna, which
is the sharp, precise, biting aspect of space, like crisp,
cold winter air: clear, cool, and precise. Until the sixth
bhumi, the maturation of prajna, the bodhisattva's actions reflect subtle attitudes. The bodhisattva does not
have enough clarity and "awakeness" to see through
them. Prajna cuts through the pieties of the bodhisattva's
approach—being extraordinarily compassionate, being
smooth and skillful, able to handle any situation, the
syrupy, honey-like quality of the bodhisattva, being
sweet and kind and gentle and at the same time slippery.
Prajna cuts through any subtle attitude, any sense of
virtue or manipulation, any sense of fixed concepts.

As the cutting through process of prajna develops, the
next stage, the seventh bhumi, also begins to unfold—
upaya or "skillful means," the perfect application of
method. In the earlier bhumis the bodhisattva's actions
—generosity, patience and so forth—were skillful, but
there was an element of piety, some sense of gratification,
of acknowledging that one's practice has fulfilled its
function. So there is a very faint but fundamental expectation in the first six bhumis. Of course, the sense of
"this and that" is not as heavy and clumsy as with those
who are not bodhisattvas, but at the same time, the
bodhisattva's neuroses are also spiritually materialistic.

They are very gentle, very slippery and difficult to catch because they contain non-duality as well as falsehood. It tends to get very complicated at this level; the more perfect you become, the subtler your imperfection. So the development of "skillful means" signifies fully stepping out of spiritual materialism. Skillful means involves using the cutting through method of prajna as well as developing a sense of the absence of "me" and "that." In other words, there is less sense of journey, less sense of a reference or checking point. You are completely tuned into what is happening on a larger scale.

Developing upaya is not so much a matter of overcoming something as it is a matter of gaining extra confidence, total confidence without a reference point. Just fully being skillful involves total lack of inhibition. We are not afraid to be. We are not afraid to live. We must accept ourselves as being warriors. If we acknowledge ourselves as warriors, then there is a way in, because a warrior dares to *be*, like a tiger in the jungle.

The Approach to Enlightenment

THE PARAMITA OF the eighth bhumi is *monlam* (*smon lam*) in Tibetan or *pranidhana* in Sanskrit, which literally means "wishful thinking" or "best wishes." Monlam means inspiration, a vision of how future developments might occur. It does not refer to wishful thinking in the ordinary sense of speculation as to what might plausibly happen in the future. This inspiration or greater vision refers to future in the sense of the pregnant aspect of the present, the present possibilities for the future. It is a very realistic approach, relating to the present as a stepping stone that contains the potential of the future.

The inspiration of the eighth bhumi is derived from relating to what is, what we are. We are inspired to walk on the broad, complete mahayana path, to deal with the world on a larger scale, a cosmic scale. The present state of being contains past and future as well.

The bodhisattva at this stage is extraordinarily confident but not in a self-centered way. His point of reference is not himself but the totality of sentient beings, so he loses track of "this" and "that." Perhaps he and all sentient beings are one and the same, so he gives up keeping track of who is who, what is what, not with blind faith or through confusion, but realistically, because there is no point in carving out territories. The future situation is there, the present situation is here, because it is so.

The paramita of the ninth bhumi is *bala* in Sanskrit or *top* (*stobs*) in Tibetan, which means "power." Power in this sense is a further expression of the confidence of skillful means. Skillful means is the confidence to step up to the edge of a cliff and power is the confidence to leap. It seems to be a very daring decision, but since there is no reference point, it is an extraordinarily ordinary situation; you simply do it. In a sense, it is much easier than self-consciously making a cup of tea.

At the beginning of the bodhisattva path there is the

tremendous joy of realizing that we have all kinds of richness and skill, that we are a total human being. Beyond that level the journey is not self-conscious, but still the unself-consciousness becomes another kind of self-consciousness. We are still using reference points, in a transcendental way of course, but we are nevertheless confirming our experience. And then, beyond the seventh bhumi, we begin to break through this barrier by experiencing complete skillful means. Finally we do not have to make a reference, we do not have to make a journey at all. Our path becomes an evolutionary process in which further power begins to develop, complete power, enlightened power. Which leads into the tenth bhumi, *dharmamegha* or dharma cloud, the development of the paramita of *yeshe* (Tibetan: *ye shes*), or wisdom (Sanskrit: *jnana*).

Wisdom is non-identification with the teaching, non-identification with the path, non-identification with the technique. The bodhisattva doesn't identify with the path any longer because he has *become* the path. He *is* the path. He has worked on himself, trod on himself, until he has become the path and the chariot as well as the occupant of the chariot, all at the same time. He is vision, energy, skillful means, generosity, knowledge, panoramic awareness. It is unspeakably powerful, and yet at the same time the bodhisattva is powerless when he is in the tenth bhumi, because he is completely programmed by the Buddha's way. This might sound paradoxical, but it is so.

There is a story of a king in India whose court soothsayers told him that within seven days there would be a rain whose water would produce madness. The king collected and stored enormous amounts of fresh water,

so that when the rain of madness fell, all of his subjects
went mad except himself. But after a while he realized
that he could not communicate with his subjects because they took the mad world to be real and could
smoothly function in the world created by their mutual
madness. So finally the king decided to abandon his
supply of fresh water and drink the water of madness.
It is a rather disappointing way of expressing the realization of enlightenment, but it is a very powerful state-
ment. When we decide to drink the water of madness,
then we have no reference point. So from that point of
view, total enlightenment is total madness. But there
is still a king and his subjects and they must run the
world together. Running the world becomes an expression of sanity because there is no reference point against
which to fight. There is something logical about the
whole bodhisattva process but something extraordinarily
illogical about it as well.

VII
Devotion

Surrendering

AT FIRST DEVOTION is inspired by a sense of inadequacy. We begin to realize that we are not up to coping with life or that we are confused about it. Even the little lighthouses we might have in the midst of our darkness seem quite vulnerable. So devotion in the hinayana stage comes from a sense of poverty. We take refuge in the buddha, dharma and sangha because we feel trapped in the problems of life. We have failed to make a comfortable nest. We want to change our claustrophobic and painful world.

You might say that certain people approach the path from more positive inspirations. They might have had a dream or a vision or an insight that inspired them to search more deeply. Possibly they had money to fly to India or the charm and courage to hitchhike there. Then they had all sorts of exotic and exciting experiences. Someone stuck in New York City might consider it a rich and heroic journey. But fundamentally such people still have the mentality of poverty. Although their initial inspiration may have been expansive, still they are uncertain about how to relate to the teachings. They feel that the teachings are too precious, too rich for them to digest. They doubt whether they can master a spiritual discipline. The more inadequate they feel, the more devoted they become. Fundamentally, such devotion involves valuing the object of devotion. The poorer you feel, the richer the guru seems by contrast. As the seeming gap between what he has and what you have grows, your devotion grows as well. You are more willing to give something to your guru.

But what do you want in return? That is the problem. "I want to be saved from pain, my misery, my problems. I would like to be saved so that I might be happy. I want to feel glorious, fantastic, good, creative. I want to be like my guru. I want to incorporate his admirable qualities into my personality. I want to enrich my ego. I want to get some new information into my system so that I might handle myself better." But this is like asking for a transplant of some kind. "Maybe the Heart of the Great Wisdom could be transplanted into my chest. Perhaps I could exchange my brain." Before we wholeheartedly give ourselves to serving a guru we should be very suspicious of why we are doing it. What are we looking for, really?

You may approach a spiritual friend and declare your intention to surrender to him. "I am dedicated to your cause, which I love very much. I love you and your teachings. Where do I sign my name? Is there a dotted line that I could sign on?" But the spiritual friend has none—no dotted line. You feel uncomfortable. "If it is an organization, why don't they have a place for me to sign my name, some way to acknowledge that I have joined them? They have discipline, morality, a philosophy but no place for me to sign my name." "As far as this organization is concerned, we do not care what your name is. Your commitment is more important than putting down your name." You might feel disturbed that you will not get some form of credentials. "Sorry, we don't need your name or address or telephone number. Just come and practice."

This is the starting point of devotion—trusting a situation in which you do not have an ID card, in which there is no room for credits or acknowledgment. Just give in. Why do we have to know who gave in? The giver needs no name, no credentials. Everybody jumps into a gigantic cauldron. It does not matter how or when you jump into it, but sooner or later you must. The water is boiling, the fire is kept going. You become part of a huge stew. The starting point of devotion is to dismantle your credentials. You need discoloring, depersonalizing of your individuality. The purpose of surrender is to make everyone grey—no white, no blue—pure grey. The teaching demands that everyone be thrown into the big cauldron of soup. You cannot stick your neck out and say, "I'm an onion, therefore I should be more smelly." "Get down, you're just another vegetable." "I'm a carrot, isn't my orange color noticeable?" "No, you are still orange only because we haven't boiled you long enough."

At this point you might say to yourself, "He's warning me to be very suspicious of how I approach the spiritual path, but what about questioning him? How do I know that what he is saying is true?" You don't. There is no insurance policy. In fact, there is much reason to be highly suspicious of me. You never met Buddha. You have only read books that others have written about what he said. Assuming that Buddha knew what was true, which of course is itself open to question, we do not know whether his message was transmitted correctly and completely from generation to generation. Perhaps

someone misunderstood and twisted it. And the message
we receive is subtly but fundamentally wrong. How do
we know that what we are hearing is actually trust-
worthy? Perhaps we are wasting our time or being misled.
Perhaps we are involved in a fraud. There is no answer
to such doubts, no authority that can be trusted. Ulti-
mately, we can trust only in our own basic intelligence.

Since you are at least considering the possibility of
trusting what I am saying, I will go on to suggest certain
guidelines for determining whether your relationship
with a teacher is genuine. Your first impulse might be
to look for a one-hundred-percent enlightened being,
someone who is recognized by the authorities, who is
famous, who seems to have helped people we know. The
trouble with that approach is that it is very difficult to
understand what qualities an enlightened being would
have. We have preconceptions as to what they are, but
do they correspond to reality? Selecting a spiritual friend
should be based upon our personal experience of communication with this person, rather than upon whether
or not the person fits our preconceptions. Proper transmission requires intimate friendship, direct contact with
the spiritual friend. If we see the guru as someone who
possesses higher, superior knowledge, who is greater than
us, who is extremely compassionate to actually pay attention to us, then transmission is blocked. If we feel that
we are a miserable little person who is being given a
golden cup, then we are overwhelmed by the gift, we
do not know what to do with it. Our gift becomes a burden because our relationship is awkward and heavy.

In the case of genuine friendship between teacher and
student there is direct and total communication which
is called "the meeting of the two minds." The teacher
opens and you open; both of you are in the same space.

In order for you to make friends with a teacher in a complete sense, he has to know what you are and how you are. Revealing that is surrendering. If your movements are clumsy or if your hands are dirty when you shake hands, you should not be ashamed of it. Just present yourself as you are. Surrendering is presenting a complete psychological portrait of yourself to your friend, including all your negative, neurotic traits. The point of meeting with the teacher is not to impress him so that he will give you something, but the point is just to present what you are. It is similar to a physician-patient relationship. You must tell your doctor what is wrong with you, what symptoms you have. If you tell him all your symptoms, then he can help you as much as possible. Whereas if you try to hide your illness, try to impress him with how healthy you are, how little attention you need, then naturally you are not going to receive much help. So to begin with devotion means to be what you are, to share yourself with a spiritual friend.

Spiritual Friend

IN THE HINAYANA Buddhist approach to devotion you are confused and need to relate to a model of sanity, to a sensible human being who, because of his disciplined practice and study, sees the world clearly. It is as if you are flipping in and out of hallucinations, so you seek out someone who can distinguish for you what is real and what is illusion. In that sense the person you

seek must be like a parent educating a child. But he is
the kind of parent who is open to communicate with you.
And like a parent, he seems to be an ordinary human
being who grew up experiencing difficulties, who shares
your concerns and your common physical needs. The
hinayanists view Buddha as an ordinary human being, a
son of man who through great perseverence attained enlightenment but who still had a body and could still
share our common human experience.

In contrast to the hinayana view of the teacher as a
parental figure, the mahayanists view the teacher as a
spiritual friend—*kalyanamitra* in Sanskrit—which literally means "spiritual friend" or "companion in the virtue." Virtue, as it is used here, is inherent richness,
rich soil fertilized by the rotting manure of neurosis. You
have tremendous potential, you are ripe, you smell like
one-hundred-percent ripe blue cheese, which can be
smelled miles away. Devotion is the acknowledging of
that potential by both the teacher and the student. The
student is like an adolescent who obviously has great
potential talents but who does not know the ways of the
world. He needs a master to teach him what to do, how
to develop his talent. He is always making mistakes due
to his inexperience and needs close supervision. At the
mahayana level the spiritual friend seems to possess much
more power and understanding than you. He has mas-
tered all kinds of disciplines and techniques and knows
how to handle situations extraordinarily well. He is like
a highly skilled physician who can prescribe the right
remedies for your frequent spiritual illnesses, your continual blundering.

At the mahayana level you are not as bothered by trying to make sure your world is real: "At last I've found
solid ground, a solid footing. I have discovered the mean-

ing of reality." We begin to relax and feel comfortable. We have found out what is edible. But how do we eat? Do we eat everything at once, without discrimination? We could get a stomach upset if we combine our foods improperly. We have to open ourselves to the suggestions of the spiritual friend at this point; he begins to mind our business a great deal. At first he may be kind and gentle with us, but nevertheless there is no privacy from him; every corner is being watched. The more we try to hide, the more our disguises are penetrated. It is not necessarily because the teacher is extremely awake or a mind-reader. Rather our paranoia about impressing him or hiding from him makes our neurosis more transparent. The covering itself is transparent. The teacher acts as a mirror, which we find irritating and discomforting. It may seem at that point that the teacher is not trying to help you at all but is deliberately being provocative, even sadistic. But such overwhelming openness is real friendship.

This friendship involves a youthful and challenging relationship in which the spiritual friend is your lover. Conventionally, a lover means someone who relates with your physical passion and makes love to you and acknowledges you in that way. Another type of lover admires you generally. He would not necessarily make love to you physically, but would acknowledge or understand your beauty, your flair, your glamorousness. In the case of the spiritual friend, he is your lover in the sense that he wants to communicate with your grotesqueness as well as your beauty. Such communication is very dangerous and painful. We are unclear how to relate to it.

Such a spiritual friend is outrageously unreasonable simply because he minds your business so relentlessly. He is concerned about how you say hello, how you handle yourself coming into the room and so on. You want him to get out of your territory, he is too much. "Don't play games with me when I'm weak and vulnerable." Even if you see him when you feel strong, then you usually want him to recognize your strength, which is another vulnerability. You are looking for feedback in either case. He seems invulnerable and you feel threatened. He is like a beautifully built train coming toward you on solid tracks; there is no way to stop him. Or he is like an antique sword with a razor-sharp edge about to strike you. The heavy-handedness of the spiritual friend is both appreciated and highly irritating. His style is extremely forceful but so together, so right that you cannot challenge it. That is devotion. You admire his style so much, but you feel terrified by it. It is beautiful but it is going to crush you, cut you to pieces. Devotion in this case involves so much sharpness that you cannot even plead for mercy by claiming to be a wretched, nice little person who is devoted and prostrates to his teacher all the time and kisses his feet. Conmanship is ineffective in such a situation. The whole thing is very heavy-handed. The real function of a spiritual friend is to insult you.

The Great Warrior

AS YOU ADVANCED to the mahayana path, the spiritual friend was like a physician. At first your relationship was sympathetic, friendly, predictable. When you visited your friend he would always sit in the same chair and you would always be served the same kind of tea. The spiritual friend would do everything precisely and everything had to be done for him precisely; if you were imprecise he would caution you. Or you might have a friend who did all kinds of crazy things, but that style was also predictable. You might even expect that he would challenge you if you acted too predictably. In either case, you were afraid of the guru changing his style, of becoming truly unpredictable. You preferred to maintain the smooth, beautiful, peaceful style of communication. You were very comfortable and could trust the situation, devote yourself wholeheartedly to it, absorb yourself in it, as though you were watching a railroad train whose wheels go round and round, chug, chug, always predictable. You knew when the train would reach the station. You knew when it would leave again—chug, chug, chug—always predictable. You hoped that your friend would always be kind and noble with you.

But at some point this kind of relationship becomes stagnant; it is too indulgent and must be cut through. Your spiritual friend will sit in your chair and serve you beer instead of tea. You are confused, you feel as if the carpet had been pulled from under your feet. The regularity and predictableness of your relationship has been challenged. That is how the spiritual friend turns into a crazy-wisdom guru. He acts unexpectedly and the atmosphere of tranquility is disturbed, which is very painful. The physician becomes wild, which is terrifying. We do not want to trust a wild doctor or surgeon. But we must. We have been nursed by our parents and treated by our

physician and now we must become an adult, a real
grownup person ready to face the world. We have to become an apprentice warrior. Devotion, at this point, involves being extraordinarily accommodating to the darts
that the spiritual friend throws at you.

You have to learn to believe in the mysteries or mystical aspect of the art of war. In the vajrayana, war is not
regarded as a struggle to gain victory. War is regarded as
an occupation. The guru is the archetypical warrior who
has knowledge of war and peace. He is a great warrior
who is familiar with the mysteries of the world, with the
mystical aspect of the world. He knows how the world
functions, how situations occur and how situations can
fool you. Devotion to the guru develops with the realization of the tremendous difficulty of finding your way in
the midst of this warfare. You need to learn from a
master warrior. Warfare demands fundamental bravery
in handling situations, a willingness to fight with situations and a willingness to believe in the mysteriousness
of life.

The guru has fantastic skill in developing you and
destroying you at the same time, because the guru can
communicate with the real world, which in turn can
communicate to you either positively or negatively. That
is one of the mysteries. People refer to it as magic or
miracle, but I do not think we have a true understanding
of it. The popular idea of magic is the dream of the
comic books—Clark Kent transforming himself into Sup-
erman. But a guru will not turn you upside down or
suspend you in the air. Nor does he have a mystical
power to watch you being old and infantile at the same
time. Nor does he have the power to turn you into a
reptile to confess your sins to him and then, having con-
fessed, turn you back into a human. People would like

to have such power, of course. It would be a tremendous thrill. "I wish I had the power to turn this person into a bug so that I could step on him." We have been reading too many comic books. Mystical power can only be expressed through an extraordinarily direct relationship with what is happening, with reality. Without a sense of compassion nothing can take place. We cannot conquer the world if we desire victory over something. We must have the sense of our relatedness with the world. Otherwise, our relationship with the world is imaginary, based upon false devotion to the guru.

One must make a very direct and personal relationship with the guru. You might give twenty-million dollars to your spiritual friend whom you love dearly, but that is not enough. You must give your ego to him. The guru must receive your juice, your vital fluid. It is not enough to give him your feathers or hair or nails. You have to surrender the real core of you, the juicy part. Even if you give everything you have—your car, your clothes, your property, your money, your contact lenses, your false teeth—it is not enough. How about giving yourself, you who possess all these things? You still hang out. It is very clumsy. Particularly in the vajrayana, teachers expect you to give yourself—it is not enough to strip off your skin and flesh and pull your bones apart and your heart out. What do you have left to give then? That is the best gift of all.

We might feel proud that we gave one of our fingers to our guru: "I cut off my ear as a gift to him," or "I cut my nose as an expression of devotion to him. I hope he will take it and regard it as a sign of how serious I am about the whole thing. And I hope he will value it because it means so much to me." To the crazy wisdom guru such sacrifice is insignificant. Vajrayana surrender

is much more painful and powerful and intimate. It is
a problem of total communication; if you hold anything
back, your relationship will be false, incomplete, and
both you and your guru will know it.

Commitment

THE CRAZY WISDOM guru has tremendous power
—the power of transformation, the power of development and also the power of deadly rejection which could
destroy you. It is said that the guru should be regarded
as being like fire: if you get too close to him you get
burned; if you stay too distant you receive no warmth.
You have to keep a reasonable distance. Getting too
close means that you would like to obtain some kind of
acknowledgment that your neuroses are a valid and
serious matter, that they should be included as part of
the bargain of the spiritual unification of guru and student. But such a bargain cannot be made because your
guru will not sign his name on the dotted line.

Unfortunately, we usually think that devotion is very
safe, pleasant and a harmonious relationship to enter
into, almost like getting married. But in the devotional
relationship there is more doubt as to whether it will
continue. You wish you could keep it a secret in case it
does not work out. There is still a great deal of mystery
concerning the teachings and the teacher. In relating
with your wife or husband there is less mysteriousness.
You know each other's backgrounds and have learned

each other's habits and you begin to suspect possible boredom. But in the case of the teachings you do not suspect boredom but you do suspect tremendous possibilities of failure and danger. Whenever this distrust arises, you surrender more, you trust more blindly, and you commit your energy more to the unknown. In spite of being unknown it is secure, absolutely safe, since you are on the side of goodness or God. You are willing to fight his enemies—vice, the devil, whatever. You are linked with goodness. "If I devote myself enough, my teacher will accept me and then he will free me." That is a big problem.

We do not realize that the wrath of the goodness is tremendously powerful. It could strike us at any time. We could be hit by any little deception, which to you is only a way of speaking, but in actual fact it seems to be much more than that. You might bend the income tax laws or plead your way out of a fine for a traffic violation, but it is not so easy with spirituality. It is a much more subtle, very acute, very immediate, very sensitive situation. When minds tune into subtle situations, then the consequences become subtle as well. The usual expectation is that when we tune our minds into a subtle situation, we get subtle pleasure out of it and can ignore the subtle pain. But both pleasurable and painful messages are equally potent.

What I am trying to say is that devotion to a teacher involves tremendous consequences. Reading this in itself can be dangerous. You are surrendering yourself, acknowledging that you have some kind of commitment. And if you go so far as to regard yourself as a student of spirituality, then you are not only siding with the goodness of the teaching but you are also embedding yourself into the soil of the teaching. Each time you fold your hands and bow, each time the teacher acknowledges your commitment, each time you light candles or incense at a shrine or sit in a meditation hall, you are rooting yourself more deeply. It is like planting a tree. Each time you water the plant, the roots grow further into the ground. Devotion is usually regarded as inconsequential. You bow and you get what you want. If you do not get it, you can walk away without any difficulty. Not so. Each bow creates a stronger umbilical cord. You become more deeply rooted in the teaching and more deeply rooted in the debt you have to repay to all sentient beings. It is extraordinarily demanding. Not realizing this is comparable to saying, "I'm doing the landlord a favor by moving into his property and signing a lease. I am doing him a favor so that he can make money from me." But you do not realize the consequence, that you are committed to pay rent as long as the lease is in effect. It is ordinary common logic.

Even if you try to pull yourself out of the relationship, some link will remain; you cannot completely undo your past. You cannot really leave without being touched. It is a terrible trap in that sense, an extraordinarily haunting thing. So realize what you are doing.

The Universality of Guru

DISCIPLINE GOES hand in hand with devotion. They are both important to each other. We could say that discipline and devotion are like the two wings of a bird. Without both of them together there is no way to relate to the spiritual friend, teacher or warrior. And without a spiritual friend there is no way to realize the teachings. And without the teachings there is no way of developing basic sanity. And without basic sanity there is no journey, no movement, there is no creative energy.

One of the problems of spiritual searching is that we tend to feel that we can help ourselves purely by reading a lot and practicing by ourselves, not associating ourselves with a particular lineage. Without a teacher to surrender to, without an object of devotion, we cannot free ourselves from spiritual materialism.

It is important first to develop a sense of devotion that allows us to be disowned by our ego. Devotion is a process of unlearning. If there is no devotion, no surrendering, we cannot unlearn. Of course we could say that sometimes even having a spiritual friend might generate further spiritual materialism as well. But it depends on the qualities of the friend and the communication of the student, whether a link is properly made or not. It is possible that a spiritual friend who is highly evolved could meet an embryonically highly-evolved person and not form a proper link. Their chemistry together must produce a spark.

Each of the approaches to devotion that we have talked about has its place. We cannot begin immediately with the vajrayana devotional approach. It would be suicidal. It would be like an infant trying to imitate a grownup. The various styles of devotion are not just progressive stages of development. They are also different aspects of each stage of development. One minute you might need a parental figure, another minute you feel sick and need a physician, another minute you might need warrior-like encouragement.

Nevertheless, we must start with the hinayana version of devotion which contains elements of the sympathy of the mahayana approach and the bravery of the vajrayana approach. But the external acts are predominantly hinayanist. Each stage along the path has its dominant themes. The hinayana approach to devotion is predominantly a simple relationship with your spiritual friend, a human relationship. The spiritual friend is not regarded as a god, saint or angel, but he is regarded as a human being who has gone through tremendous discipline and learning. We can identify with this person because we can communicate with him. He is not a Martian who is pretending to be an earthman, but he is a son of man who grew up in this world and experienced all kinds of difficulties and was able to relate with the teaching and accomplish tremendous things. We can relate with this person without fantasizing all kinds of mysteries.

The hinayanist approach is very matter of fact: you are relating to another human being who happens to be accomplished. And the mahayanist approach is that this person is so highly accomplished that he is extraordinarily in tune with the events of everyday life. He has a perfectly constant awareness so that he does not miss a point. And he has developed exceedingly powerful compassion to live through your negativities. Your trying to walk on the spiritual path may be a big joke to your spiritual friend. You may act as an absolutely confused and absurd person. Nevertheless this person never gives up hope for you. He accepts you and goes through the irritations that you create. He is tremendously patient with you. You do something wrong and he instructs you how to correct it. But then you slip up or distort the instruction; you create further mistakes. You go back to your spiritual friend and he says, "Fine, we can still work together, but now try this project," and you try again. You start with tremendous energy and confidence that you can do it. Several days later you get tired of the whole thing. You find something else with which to entertain yourself. The spiritual friend might ask you to do an intensive meditation practice without reading books, but you find that a book jumps into your lap and you cannot help reading it. It seems to be a part of the teaching as well. And you go back to the spiritual friend and say, "I followed your instructions but this book jumped into my lap and I could not help reading it." The spiritual friend then says, "That's fine. Did you learn anything from it? If you did, take the book and keep reading, find out what the book has to say in depth." And you go back and try to read the book, but you tire of reading. It's springtime. The flowers and trees and nature are so glamorous that you cannot help putting the book aside and taking a nice walk, enjoying the beauty of nature and the "meditative" state of being in nature. Following discipline is very difficult and you constantly create sidetracks by not realizing that you are sidetracking. The problem is not that you disobey your spiritual friend. In fact, the problem is that you are too serious; you find your sidetracks by being very serious. So it requires tremendous patience for your spiritual friend to work with you despite your slipping in and out of disciplines, despite your frivolousness.

A bodhisattva is like a crocodile: once you land in its mouth it never lets you go. If you were to want to leave your spiritual friend in order to live a free life away from such involvement, he would say, "That's great, do as you wish, go ahead and leave." By approving your leaving he removes the object of your rebellion, so instead of going away you come closer. It is a reciprocal situation: the guru's devotion to the student is intense and therefore the student's devotion begins to awaken, even if he is stupid and thick and burdened with all kinds of problems. The teacher's devotion to the student is compassion and the devotion of the student to the teacher is discipline. So compassion and discipline begin to meet together at some point.

And then we come to the vajrayana type of devotion in which you have given up fascination. You have identified with the path and the phenomenal world becomes an expression of the guru. There is a sense of devotion to the phenomenal world. You finally identify with the teachings and occasionally you act as a spokesman for them. Even to your own subconscious mind you act as their spokesman. If we are able to reach this level, then any events which occur in life have messages in them, have teachings in them. Teachings are everywhere. This is not a simple-minded notion of magic in the sense of gadgetry or trickery, but it is an astounding situation which you could interpret as magic. There is cause and effect involved. The events of your life act as a spokesman constantly and you cannot get away from this guru; in fact you do not want to because you identify with it. Thus the teachings become less claustrophobic, which enables you to discover the magical quality of life situations as a teaching.

Generally, devotion is regarded as coming from the heart rather than the head. But tantric devotion involves the head as well as the heart. For instance, *The Tibetan Book of the Dead* uses the symbolism of the peaceful deities coming out of your heart and the wrathful deities coming from your head. The vajrayana approach is a head approach—head plus heart together. The hinayana and mahayana approaches to devotion come from the heart. The tantric approach to life is intellectual in some sense because you begin to read the implications behind things. You begin to see messages that wake you up. But at the same time that intellect is not based upon speculation but is felt wholeheartedly, with one-hundred-percent heart. So we could say that the tantric approach to the messages of the all-pervading guru is to begin with intellect, which is transmuted into vajra intellect, and that begins to ignite the intuition of the heart at the same time.

This is the ideal fundamental union of prajna and shunyata, the union of eyes and heart together. Everyday events become self-existing teachings. Even the notion of trust does not apply any more. You might ask, "Who is doing this trusting?" Nobody! Trust itself is trusting itself. The mandala of self-existing energy does not have to be maintained by anything at all; it maintains itself. Space does not have a fringe or a center. Each corner of space is center as well as fringe. That is the all-pervading devotion in which the devotee is not separate from the object of devotion.

But before we indulge too much in such exciting and mystical language, we have to start very simply by giving, opening, displaying our ego, making a gift of our ego to our spiritual friend. If we are unable to do this, then the path never begins because there is nobody to walk on it. The teaching exists but the practitioner must acknowledge the teaching, must embody it.

VIII
Tantra

Aloneness

THE SPIRITUAL PATH is not fun—better not be-
gin it. If you must begin, then go all the way, because if
you begin and quit, the unfinished business you have
left behind begins to haunt you all the time. The path,
as Suzuki Roshi mentions in *Zen Mind, Beginner's Mind,*
is like getting on-to a train that you cannot get off; you
ride it on and on and on. The mahayana scriptures com-
pare the bodhisattva vow of acceptance of the path to
planting a tree. So stepping on the path involves you in
continual growth, which may be tremendously painful
since you sometimes try to step off the path. You do not
really want to get into it fully; it is too close to the heart.
And you are not able to trust in the heart. Your experiences become too penetrating, too naked, too obvious.
Then you try to escape, but your avoidance creates pain
which in turn inspires you to continue on the path. So
your setbacks and suffering are part of the creative process of the path.

The continuity of the path is expressed in the ideas
of ground tantra, path tantra and fruition tantra. Ground
tantra is acknowledging the potential that exists within
you, that you are part of buddha-nature, otherwise you
would not be able to appreciate the teachings. And it

acknowledges your starting point, your confusion and pain. Your suffering is truth; it is intelligent. The path tantra involves developing an attitude of richness and generosity. Confusion and pain are viewed as sources of inspiration, a rich resource. Furthermore, you acknowledge that you are intelligent and courageous, that you are able to be fundamentally alone. You are willing to have an operation without the use of anesthetics, constantly unfolding, unmasking, opening on and on and on. You are willing to be a lonely person, a desolate person, are willing to give up the company of your shadow, your twenty-four-hour-a-day commentator who follows you constantly, the watcher.

In the Tibetan tradition the watcher is called *dzinba* (*'dzin pa*), which means "fixation" or "holding." If we give up the watcher, then we have nothing left for which to survive, nothing left for which to continue. We give up hope of holding on to something. That is a very big step toward true asceticism. You have to give up the questioner and the answer—that is, discursive mind, the checking mechanism that tells you whether you are doing well or not doing well. "I am this, I am that." "Am I doing all right, am I meditating correctly, am I studying well, am I getting somewhere?" If we give all this up, then how do we know if we are advancing in spiritual practice? Quite possibly there is no such thing as spiritual practice except stepping out of self-deception, stopping our struggle to get hold of spiritual states. Just give that up. Other than that there is no spirituality. It is a very desolate situation. It is like living among snow-capped peaks with clouds wrapped around them and the sun and moon starkly shining over them. Below, tall alpine trees are swayed by strong, howling winds and beneath them is a thundering waterfall. From our point of view, we may appreciate this desolation if we are an occasional tourist who photographs it or a mountain climber trying to climb to the mountain top. But we do not really want to live in those desolate places. It's no fun. It is terrifying, terrible.

But it is possible to make friends with the desolation and appreciate its beauty. Great sages like Milarepa relate to the desolation as their bride. They marry themselves to desolation, to the fundamental psychological aloneness. They do not need physical or psychological entertainment. Aloneness becomes their companion, their spiritual consort, part of their being. Wherever they go they are alone, whatever they do they are alone. Whether they relate socially with friends or meditate alone or perform ceremonies together or meditate together, aloneness is there all the time. That aloneness is freedom, fundamental freedom. The aloneness is described as the marriage of shunyata and wisdom in which your perception of aloneness suggests the needlessness of dualistic occupation. It is also described as the marriage of shunyata and compassion in which aloneness inspires compassionate action in living situations. Such a discovery reveals the possibility of cutting through the karmic chain reactions that recreate ego-oriented situations, because that aloneness or the space of desolation does not entertain you, does not feed you anymore. Ultimate asceticism becomes part of your basic nature. We discover how samsaric occupations feed and entertain us. Once we see samsaric occupations as games, then that in itself is the absence of dualistic fixation, nirvana. Searching for nirvana becomes redundant at that point.

So at the beginning of the path we accept our basic

qualities, which is ground tantra, and then we tread the path, which could be hot or cold, pleasurable or painful. In fruition tantra, which is beyond what we have discussed, we discover our basic nature. The whole process of the spiritual path, from the Buddhist point of view, is an organic one of natural growth: acknowledging the ground as it is, acknowledging the chaos of the path, acknowledging the colorful aspect of the fruition. The whole process is an endless odyssey. Having attained realization, one does not stop at that point, but one continues on, endlessly expressing buddha activity.

Mandala

WE FOUND THAT in the mahayana or bodhisattva path there is still some kind of effort involved, not necessarily the effort of the heavy-handed ego, but there is still some kind of self-conscious notion that "I am practicing this, I am putting my effort into this." You know exactly what to do, there is no hesitation, action happens very naturally, but some solid quality of ego is still present in a faint way. At that stage a person's experience of shunyata meditation is very powerful, but still there is a need to relate to the universe more directly. This requires a leap rather than a disciplined effort, a generosity in the sense of willingness to open yourself to the phenomenal world, rather than merely being involved with a strategy of how to relate with it. Strategy becomes irrelevant and the actual perception of energy becomes more important.

One must transcend the ego's strategies—aggression, passion and ignorance—and become completely one with those energies. We do not try to remove or destroy them, but we transmute their basic nature. This is the approach of the vajrayana, the tantric or yogic path. The word "yoga" means "union," complete identification, not only with the techniques of meditation and skillful, compassionate communication, but also with the energies that exist within the universe.

The word "tantra" means "continuity." The continuity of development along the path and the continuity of life experience becomes clearer and clearer. Every insight becomes a confirmation. The symbolism inherent in what we perceive becomes naturally relevant rather than being another fascinating or interesting imposition from outside, as though it were something we had never known about before. Visual symbolism, the sound symbolism of mantra and the mental symbolism of feeling, of energy, all become relevant. Discovering a new way of looking at experience does not become a strain or too potent; it is a natural process. Complete union with the energy of the universe and seeing the relationships of things to each other as well as the vividness of things as they are is the *mandala* principle.

"Mandala" is a Sanskrit word which means "society," "group," "association." It implies that everything is centered around something. In the case of the tantric version of mandala, everything is centered around centerless space in which there is no watcher or perceiver. Because there is no watcher or perceiver, the fringe becomes extremely vivid. The mandala principle expresses the ex-

perience of seeing the relatedness of all phenomena, that
there is a continual cycle of one experience leading to
the next. The patterns of phenomena become clear because there is no partiality in one's perspective. All
corners are visible, awareness is all-pervading.

The mandala principle of complete identification with
aggression, passion and ignorance is realized by practice
of the father tantra, the mother tantra, and the union
tantra. The father tantra is associated with aggression
or repelling. By transmuting aggression, one experiences
an energy that contains tremendous force. No confusion
can enter into it; confusion is automatically repelled. It
is called "vajra anger" since it is the diamond-like aspect
of energy. Mother tantra is associated with seduction or
magnetizing which is inspired by discriminating wisdom.
Every texture of the universe or life is seen as containing
a beauty of its own. Nothing is rejected and nothing is
accepted but whatever you perceive has its own individual qualities. Because there is no rejection or acceptance, therefore the individual qualities of things
become more obvious and it is easier to relate with
them. Therefore discriminating wisdom appreciates the
richness of every aspect of life. It inspires dancing with
phenomena. This magnetizing is a sane version of passion. With ordinary passion we try to grasp one particular highlight of a situation and ignore the rest of the
area in which that highlight is located. It is as if we try
to catch a fish with a hook but are oblivious to the ocean
in which the fish swims. Magnetizing in the case of
mother tantra is welcoming every situation but with discriminating wisdom. Everything is seen precisely as it
is, and thus there is no conflict. It does not bring indi-
gestion. Union tantra involves transmuting ignorance

into all-pervading space. In ordinary ignorance we try to maintain our individuality by ignoring our environment. But in the union tantra there is no maintenance of individuality. It is perception of the whole background of space, which is the opposite of the frozen space of ignorance.

To transmute aggression, passion and ignorance one must be able to communicate with energy directly and completely, without strategizing. Someone who is involved with a completely open attitude to the universe does not have to try to work these things out intellectually or even intuitively by effort, but the orders of the universe are obvious to him. Whatever he perceives speaks to him. Often it is said in the scriptures that all sight is the visual mandala, all sound is the mantra mandala, all thought is *citta* mandala, and the essence of consciousness is space. A person who perceives these mandalas does not see deities dancing around with strange mantras echoing, nor does he see space with all sorts of psychic flashes occurring in his mind. Such notions are a kindergarten view of heaven. If we literally see colors and shapes and hear mantras echoing in space and take note of them, we are actually confirming our ego. Quite likely we could get tired of hearing them and seeing them. Sooner or later we would want to run away from them, they would become too much, too constant. One might prefer to go to hell rather than remain in heaven. Hell might seem more exciting, more rugged.

In the ultimate experience of mandala the simple colors and shapes are metaphors. Of course if you see very vivid passion, you could paint a picture of it with all sorts of flames and ornaments. It is very interesting that tantric practitioners in India created an icono-

graphic structure with divinities clothed in classical
Indian royal costumes with turbans and crowns and
jewels and rainbow-colored clothing. While in China,
the tantric practitioners depicted deities wearing Chinese imperial dress, long brocade robes with big sleeves;
they are seen with big moustaches and holding Chinese
scepters. One might ask which depiction is more accurate. The Indians would say, "Ours is more accurate
because we perceived it that way, we imagined it that
way," and the Chinese would claim the same. We could
say that both are accurate, and both are also inaccurate.

On the whole, understanding the vividness of the
energy of the universe in terms of symbolism, in terms
of patterns, colors and shapes, is not a matter of imagination or hallucination for the real tantric practitioner.
It is real. It is similar to a person hearing music that is
very moving to him and feeling that he could almost
carve statues out of it, that he could almost hold it,
handle it. Sound becomes almost a solid object, almost a
color or a shape. If a person is able to see the energies
of the universe as they are, then shapes and colors and
patterns suggest themselves; symbolism happens. That is
the meaning of *mahamudra,* which means "great symbol." The whole world is symbol—not symbol in the
sense of a sign representing something other than itself,
but symbol in the sense of the highlights of the vivid
qualities of things as they are.

Mahamudra Upadesa

ORAL INSTRUCTIONS ON Mahamudra Given by
Sri Tilopa to Naropa at the Banks of the Ganges River.
Translated from the Sanskrit into Tibetan by *Chokyi-
Lodro* (*Chos kyi bLo gros*) Marpa the Translator.

Homage to the Co-emergent Wisdom![1]

Mahamudra cannot be shown;
But for you who are devoted to the guru, who have
    mastered the ascetic practices
And are forbearant in suffering, intelligent Naropa,
Take this to heart, my fortunate student.

Kye-ho![2]

Look at the nature of the world,
Impermanent like a mirage or dream;
Even the mirage or dream does not exist.
Therefore, develop renunciation and abandon worldly
    activities.

Renounce servants and kin, causes of passion and aggres-
    sion.
Meditate alone in the forest, in retreats, in solitary places.

157

Remain in the state of non-meditation.
If you attain non-attainment, then you have attained
mahamudra.

The dharma[3] of samsara is petty, causing passion and
aggression.
The things we have created have no substance; therefore,
seek the substance of the ultimate.
The dharma of mind cannot see the meaning of transcendent mind.
The dharma of action cannot discover the meaning of
non-action.

If you would attain the realization of transcendent mind
and non-action,
Then cut the root of mind and let consciousness remain
naked.
Let the polluted waters of mental activities clear.
Do not seek to stop projections, but let them come to
rest of themselves.
If there is no rejecting or accepting, then you are liberated in the mahamudra.

When trees grow leaves and branches,
If you cut the roots, the many leaves and branches wither.
Likewise, if you cut the root of mind,
The various mental activities will subside.

The darkness that has collected in thousands of *kalpas*[4]
One torch will dispel.
Likewise, one moment's experience of luminous mind
Will dissolve the veil of karmic impurities.

Men of lesser intelligence who cannot grasp this,
Concentrate your awareness and focus on the breath.
Through different eye-gazes and concentration practices,
Discipline your mind until it rests naturally.

If you perceive space,
The fixed ideas of center and boundary dissolve.
Likewise, if mind perceives mind,
All mental activities will cease, you will remain in a
    state of non-thought,
And you will realize the supreme *bodhi-citta*.[5]

Vapors arising from the earth become clouds and then
    vanish into the sky;
It is not known where the clouds go when they have
    dissolved.
Likewise, the waves of thoughts derived from mind
Dissolve when mind perceives mind.

Space has neither color nor shape;
It is changeless, it is not tinged by black or white.
Likewise, luminous mind has neither color nor shape;
It is not tinged by black or white, virtue or vice.

The sun's pure and brilliant essence
Cannot be dimmed by the darkness that endures for a
    thousand kalpas.
Likewise, the luminous essence of mind
Cannot be dimmed by the long kalpas of samsara.

Though it may be said that space is empty,
Space cannot be described.
Likewise, though it may be said that mind is luminous,

Naming it does not prove that it exists.
Space is completely without locality.
Likewise, mahamudra mind dwells nowhere.

Without change, rest loose in the primordial state;
There is no doubt that your bonds will loosen.
The essence of mind is like space;
Therefore, there is nothing which it does not encompass.

Let the movements of the body ease into genuineness,
Cease your idle chatter, let your speech become an echo,
Have no mind, but see the dharma of the leap.

The body, like a hollow bamboo, has no substance.
Mind is like the essence of space, having no place for
   thoughts.
Rest loose your mind; neither hold it nor permit it to
   wander.
If mind has no aim, it is mahamudra.
Accomplishing this is the attainment of supreme en-
   lightenment.

The nature of mind is luminous, without object of perception.
You will discover the path of Buddha when there is no
   path of meditation.
By meditating on non-meditation you will attain the
   supreme bodhi.[6]

This is the king of views—it transcends fixing and
   holding.[7]
This is the king of meditations—without wandering
   mind.

This is the king of actions—without effort.
When there is no hope and fear, you have realized the
goal.

The unborn *alaya*[8] is without habits and veils.
Rest mind in the unborn essence; make no distinctions
between meditation and post-meditation.
When projections exhaust the dharma of mind,
One attains the king of views, free from all limitations.

Boundless and deep is the supreme king of meditations.
Effortless self-existence is the supreme king of actions.
Hopeless self-existence is the supreme king of the
fruition.

In the beginning mind is like a turbulent river.
In the middle it is like the River Ganges, flowing slowly.
In the end it is like the confluence of all rivers, like the
meeting of son and mother.

The followers of Tantra, the *Prajnaparamita,*
The Vinaya,[9] the Sutras, and other religions—
All these, by their texts and philosophical dogmas,
Will not see the luminous mahamudra.

Having no mind, without desires,
Self-quieted, self-existing,
It is like a wave of water.
Luminosity is veiled only by the rising of desire.

The real vow of *samaya*[10] is broken by thinking in terms
of precepts.
If you neither dwell, perceive, nor stray from the ultimate,

Then you are the holy practitioner, the torch which illumines darkness.

If you are without desire, if you do not dwell in extremes,
You will see the dharmas of all the teachings.

If you strive in this endeavor, you will free yourself from samsaric imprisonment.
If you meditate in this way, you will burn the veil of karmic impurities.
Therefore, you are known as "The Torch of the Doctrine."

Even ignorant people who are not devoted to this teaching
Could be saved by you from constantly drowning in the river of samsara.

It is a pity that beings endure such suffering in the lower realms.
Those who would free themselves from suffering should seek a wise guru.
Being possessed by the *adhishthana*,[11] one's mind will be freed.

If you seek a *karma mudra*,[12] then the wisdom of the union of joy and emptiness will arise.
The union of skillful means and knowledge brings blessings.
Bring it down and give rise to the mandala.
Deliver it to the places and distribute it throughout the body.

If there is no desire involved, then the union of joy and
  emptiness will arise.
Gain long life, without white hairs, and you will wax like
  the moon.
Become radiant, and your strength will be perfect.
Having speedily achieved the relative *siddhis*,[13] one
  should seek the absolute siddhis.
May this pointed instruction in mahamudra remain in
  the hearts of fortunate beings.

Notes to Mahamudra Upadesa

1. Co-emergent Wisdom—The primordial wisdom, born simultaneously with ignorance, just as nirvana and samsara must
come simultaneously into being.
2. Kye-ho!—SK: Hark! or Listen!
3. dharma—here taken as law, pattern, path.
4. *kalpas*—SK: eons.
5. *bodhi-citta*—SK: awakened mind.
6. bodhi—SK: the awakened state.
7. fixing and holding—holding: holding on-to projections; fixing: believing in the existence of a projector.
8. unborn *alaya*—SK: The *dharmadhatu*, the primordial state
beyond being and non-being.
9. *Vinaya*—SK: the scriptures containing the hinayana rules
of discipline.
10. *samaya*—SK: the tantric vows of discipline.
11. *adhishthana*—SK: blessings, the atmosphere created by
the guru.
12. *karma mudra*—SK: one's consort in the practice of the
third *abhisheka*, the third initiation.
13. *siddhis*—SK: miraculous powers.

Appendix

The Ten Bhumis and Their Corresponding Paramitas
(This organization of the Ten Bhumis and the Ten Paramitas is
taken from the Dasabhumikasutra.)

Tibetan Pronunciation	*Tibetan Spelling*	*Sanskrit*	*English*
sa	sa	bhumi	stage
pharoltu chinpa	pha rol tu phyin pa	paramita	transcendental activity

The Ten Bhumis

1. raptu gawa	rab tu dga' ba	pramudita	very joyful
2. trima mepa	dri ma med pa	vimala	stainless
3. o jepa	'od byed pa	prabhakari	luminous
4. o trowa	'od 'phro ba	arcismati	radiant
5. shintu jang kawa	shin tu sbyang dka' ba	sudurjaya	difficult to conquer
6. ngontu gyurpa	mngon du gyur pa	abhimukhi	face to face
7. ringtu songwa	ring du song ba	durangama	far going
8. mi yowa	mi g.yo ba	acala	immovable
9. legpe lotro	legs pa'i blo gros	sadhumati	having good intellect
10. chokyi trin	chos kyi sprin	dharmamegha	cloud of dharma

The Ten Paramitas

1. jinpa	sbyin pa	dana	generosity
2. tsultim	tshul khrims	sila	discipline
3. sopa	bzod pa	ksanti	patience
4. tsondru	brtson 'grus	virya	exertion
5. samten	bsam gtan	dhyana	meditation
6. sherab	shes rab	prajna	knowledge
7. thap	thabs	upaya	skillful means
8. monlam	smon lam	pranidhana	vision
9. top	stobs	bala	power
10. yeshe	ye shes	jnana	wisdom

Index